Shoeless Joe and Ragtime Baseball

Also By Harvey Frommer

Holzman on Hoops *(with Red Holzman)*

Behind the Lines *(with Don Strock)*

It Happened in the Catskills *(with Myrna Frommer)*

Running Tough *(with Tony Dorsett)*

Growing Up at Bat: The Official 50th Anniversary of Little League Baseball

Throwing Heat *(with Nolan Ryan)*

Primitive Baseball: The National Pastime in the Gilded Age

150th Anniversary Album of Baseball

Red on Red *(with Red Holzman)*

Olympic Controversies

City Tech: The First Forty Years

Baseball's Greatest Managers

National Baseball Hall of Fame

The Games of the XXIIIrd Olympiad: Official Commemorative Book *(Editor & Principal Author)*

Jackie Robinson

Baseball's Greatest Records, Streaks, and Feats

Sports Genes *(with Myrna Frommer)*

Baseball's Greatest Rivalry: The New York Yankees and the Boston Red Sox

Rickey and Robinson: The Man Who Broke Baseball's Color Line

Basketball My Way—Nancy Lieberman *(with Myrna Frommer)*

The Sports Date Book *(with Myrna Frommer)*

New York City Baseball: 1947–1957

The Great American Soccer Book

Sports Roots

Sports Lingo: A Dictionary of the Language of Sports

The Martial Arts: Judo and Karate

A Sailing Primer

A Baseball Century

Shoeless JOE and Ragtime Baseball

Harvey Frommer

Taylor Publishing Company
Dallas, Texas

Published by Taylor Publishing Company
            1550 West Mockingbird Lane
            Dallas, Texas 75235

Photos courtesy of the National Baseball Hall of Fame, the Library of Congress, and the Chicago Historical Society.

Designed by Hespenheide Design

Library of Congress Cataloging-in-Publication Data

Frommer, Harvey.
    Shoeless Joe Jackson and ragtime baseball / Harvey Frommer.
        p.   cm.
    Includes index.
    ISBN 0-87833-820-9
    1. Jackson, Joe, 1888–1951.   2. Baseball players—United States—
Biography.   3. Chicago White Sox (Baseball team)—History.
4. Baseball—United States—History—20th century.   I. Title.
GV865.J29F76   1992
796.357′092—dc20   91–43040
    [B]   CIP

Printed in the United States of America

10   9   8   7   6   5   4   3

FIRST PAPERBACK PRINTING: MARCH 1993

For my son, Freddy, with much love.
One day, I know, he will dedicate a book to me.

Acknowledgments

At the top of the list is my severest critic and greatest ally—my wife Myrna. This book has her deft touch and writing insights on each and every page.

A tip of the hat goes to my excellent editor at Taylor, Jim Donovan. He was there from start to finish, capably coaching away.

Others who make the list: Virginia Stannard of the Greenville County Library, Bill Jenkinson, Wayne Cunningham, *The Sporting News,* and the National Baseball Hall of Fame.

Finally, special thanks to my son Freddy for his careful proofreading and on-target queries.

Contents

Sixteen pages of photographs follow page 114

. . . And let me speak to the yet unknowing world
How these things came about: so shall you hear . . .
Of accidental judgments, casual slaughters;
Of deaths put on by cunning and forc'd cause,
And, in this upshot, purposes mistook
Fall'n on the inventors' heads;
All this can I
Truly deliver.

William Shakespeare, *Hamlet*

Jackson's fall from grace is one of the real tragedies of baseball. I always thought he was more sinned against than sinning.

Connie Mack

Shoeless Joe and Ragtime Baseball

Prologue

Sometime in the late 1940s Ty Cobb and sportswriter Grantland Rice stopped off at a liquor store in Greenville, South Carolina, on their way back from the Masters Golf Tournament in Augusta, Georgia.

Cobb greeted the heavyset man behind the counter. "I know you," he said. "You're Joe Jackson. Don't you know me, Joe? I came by especially to say hello."

"I know you," said the man behind the counter, "but I wasn't sure you wanted to speak to me. A lot of them don't."

When the two men had last met more than a quarter of a century earlier, it was on a baseball field. Both were celebrants then, close competitors in the rush to be the best. But life had proscribed vastly different paths for each. Cobb had become a baseball Hall of Famer, a hailed legend, a millionaire entrepreneur, while Jackson had lived in the ignominy of tarnished glory, winding down his life not far from the small town where he was born.

"Joe," said Cobb, "you had the most natural ability, the greatest swing I ever saw."

Jackson nodded and looked away for an instant.

"Could I get an autographed baseball from you?" Cobb continued. "I always wanted one."

Jackson hesitated. "I'll get you one, but you'll have to come back tomorrow if that's all right."

"Well, we're just passing through . . . we'll do it some other time."

There was never another time. It would have been easy for Jackson to get a ball that same day, but still, after all the years, he had not learned to sign his name.

[1]

Greenville

The era 1900–1920 was one of great transition for the United States. It was coming of age and becoming a world power. It was a time when baseball gave America, a land of brief history and limited mythology, a cast of characters, a saga of adventures, a substitute for the newly closed frontier. It was also when baseball high-stepped out of its nineteenth-century roots, through the era of ragtime into its role as the national pastime, from an agrarian ethos into a ritual that would become part of American life.

In doing so, it echoed the new ragtime music that was capturing the nation's attention. The first organized music to become part of the world of jazz, ragtime utilized two coronets, a trombone, a clarinet, a banjo or guitar, a tuba or string bass, and drums. It was based on formal composition, the parts flowing into the whole—yet its appeal was unmistakably modern, a sense of something new. Baseball was likewise a formal and deliberate composition, its diverse parts contributing to a regulated whole, a game of a nation on the move.

Baseball's evolvement mirrored the larger transformations of the nation: the abandonment of the restraints of the Victorian period, the closing of the frontier, mass immigration, the development of cities, growing attention to entertainment and leisure-time activities, mass production and the development of scientific management, emergent American imperialism and military might. The population of the United States increased from 76 million to 106 million during that era, and the population of its large cities escalated from 30 to 54 million.

Change and newness were everywhere. A five-cent piece featuring the buffalo and Indian head came into being. The Boy Scouts of America were formed. George Eastman built the first Kodak camera and sold it for $25. The Sears & Roebuck catalogue was introduced (one of its first products was an organ in a solid oak case that sold for $37.35) and included a money-back guarantee for any dissatisfied customers.

Average annual earnings climbed from nearly $500 at the start of the century to almost $1,500 by the end of its second decade. The workweek dropped from 57.4 hours to 50.4 hours.

Technological advances, improvements in newspaper printing, the camera, the telephone and telegraph, the motion picture—all of these brought information and entertainment more quickly to more people. You could see *The Great Train Robber*—a twelve-minute film—for five cents in a nickelodeon in 10,000 stores.

It was the time of poets like Carl Sandburg and Robert Frost, a time when people went to see such performers as Tom Mix, Charlie Chaplin, John Barrymore, Gloria Swanson, Douglas Fairbanks, and Mary Pickford, a time when Irving Berlin, Victor Herbert, and Sigmund Romberg were writing America's favorite songs.

In 1910, two billion copies of sheet music were sold. A couple of favorites were "A Bird in a Gilded Cage" and "Shine on Harvest Moon." Baseball players as composers, singers, speakers—all were part of the popular musical scene.

"The Red Sox Speed Boys," a little ditty that appeared in the mid-1900s, did very well. The title was wishful thinking, because the Sox were at or near last in stolen bases throughout those years. The "American League Two Step" was dedicated to the pennant-winning 1905 Philadelphia A's. The "White Sox March" was published in 1907 to celebrate the '06 World Champions. "Cubs on Parade," a march two-step by H.R. Hempel, was dedicated to Chicago's 1907 World Champions. A song called "Between You and Me," allegedly written by Johnny Evers and Joe Tinker, was referred to as "the catch of the season." The sport's anthem, "Take Me Out to the Ballgame," was published in 1908.

During the ragtime era Cornelius Vanderbilt built what he called a "small cottage"—a 70-room mansion that cost $5 million. William Vanderbilt spent $6 million more for a marble house. The spendings of the Vanderbilts were the exception.

In that America of forty-five states at the turn of the century there were no radios and no refrigerators; eggs were twelve cents a dozen, a complete turkey dinner cost twenty cents. At the Squirrel Inn at 131 Bowery in New York City, a family of six could eat for $1.00 and still have change left over. A steak, beef stew, or three fried eggs cost ten cents at the Squirrel Inn while for five cents you could order coffee, tea, milk or cocoa, and pie. Barber shops featured shaving mugs individually emblazoned with the names of customers. A shave was fifteen cents. You could purchase a made-to-order suit from a skilled tailor for ten dollars, a frontier 44-caliber revolver for $3.75, a Homan sewing machine for $7.58, a pocket watch for fifty-nine cents, a standard stethoscope for twenty-eight cents, an Armorside corset for eighty-five cents.

That America of 1900 was shocked by the assassination of President William McKinley. Teddy Roosevelt succeeded him, becoming the youngest president of the United States in history. He was forty-two years old.

Although Henry Ford had popularized the "Tin Lizzie" and the $5-a-day wage scale for a full eight-hour day, there were less than 10,000 cars in America of the early 1900s. Many of those who did have cars were subjected to the cry of "Get a horse" whenever there was a rainstorm and they had to struggle to get their cars out of muddy ditches in the roads.

Changing demographics altered the appearance and feel of America. The falling price of cotton, rising costs, and a public outcry against the use of child labor sent Northern mill owners south. There they built mill towns with mill stores and mill churches and mill homes. Countless small towns were overrun by the booming new industry.

Greenville, South Carolina was just such a town.

Joseph Jefferson Wofford Jackson was born on July 16, 1889 in Pickens County, not more than fifteen miles outside of Greenville, the first of six boys and two girls brought into the world by George Elmore and Martha Ann Jackson. The Jacksons were Baptists but not religious. Still, Martha Jackson, a big woman who kept her jet-black hair tied back in a knot and who was skilled in making hot biscuits and jelly from apples, refrained from cooking on Sunday.

When Joe was six years old, the family moved to Brandon, a town of about 13,000 people ringed by textile mills. There, like the others his age, Joe was put to work sweeping floors in the mill. The long stultifying hours of working as a cleanup boy, or "linthead," depressed him.

By 1902, when Joe Jackson was thirteen years old, he was working a dozen hours a day in the cotton mill along with his father and a brother and all the other mill workers who outnumbered the citizens of Greenville two to one.

The boy's sole escape from the whirring machinery and the din, dust, and danger of the mill took place out in the fields, playing baseball.

Because Southern mill workers frequently moved from town to town, job to job, the owners of the mills introduced measures to try and keep a hold on their workers, to literally "keep them in their place." Cows, organs, expensive merchandise was made available—all on credit. Organized social gatherings were staged weekly to create a sense of community. And there was also baseball. The Textile League provided a rooting interest for workers and a sense of belonging. All mill cities were interconnected by a railroad called the Belt Line. Saturday afternoons teams and their fans went from town to town for baseball. Those who played for the Textile League teams were given the easiest jobs, some time off for practice, and lots of prestige.

The managers of the Brandon Mill team had observed the gangly Joe Jackson playing baseball in pickup games or in those moments he stole away from mill work. Impressed with his natural ability, they asked Joe's mother for permission to allow him to play for their team.

The teenager was a natural right from the start, pounding homers with a baseball that was fat and soft and scuffed and heavy. "Joe's Saturday Special" was how fans referred to a Jackson home run. Each time Joe smacked a home run, his younger brothers—David, Jerry, Earl, Ernest, and Luther—would race into the stands. In a businesslike manner they would pass the hat and collect money from the fans. There were times Joe's brothers picked up as much as $25—about a good month's pay at the mill. This, coupled with the $2.50 paid to each player for the Saturday games, netted the young Joe Jackson a tidy sum, which he passed on to his mother and father.

Katie Wynn, four years younger than Jackson, was one of his most ardent fans. She rooted for Joe at the games and spent time with him at Harrison's Drugstore in Greenville. It was there that he would often order his favorite drink—"dope and lime"—a beverage whose name was far more deadly than its actual contents: Coca-Cola and a squirt of lime.

Good quality baseball gloves of the time could be purchased for about two dollars, but they were used more as protection against the ball rather than anything else. The bat was the baseball player's real tool of his trade.

Charlie Ferguson, the local batmaker, was a follower and a fan of Joe Jackson. The two would often talk bats and the art and science of fashioning the right kind. When Joe was fifteen, Charlie presented the youth with a bat that he had created from a well-seasoned four-by-four that had once been part of a strong hickory tree. The bat was ash white when it was completed, but Charlie Ferguson knew that Joe liked black bats. So the batmaker busied himself adding the finishing touches to the 36-inch long, 48-ounce bat that he shaped to the fit of Joe's large and growing hands. A couple of coats of tobacco juice transformed the bat into a glistening piece of wood with the look of ebony about it. Joe Jackson called the bat "Black Betsy."

Ferguson gave specific instruction on the care of the bat— the rubbing with sweet oil, the wrapping in a clean cotton cloth when not in use. And Joe Jackson followed these directions to the letter.

Joe's long gangling arms that had so much power in them convinced Brandon Mill officials to tinker with playing the youth at catcher. But Jackson's catching career was aborted when a pitch from a burly mill hand dented his catcher's mask into his forehead, scarring him there for life. He played a bit of third base and pitched a little. But the outfield was where he finally settled, where he was able to use his running speed and powerful arm to the greatest advantage.

It was the custom of the time for mill teams to raid and outbid each other for gifted players. That was how Joe wound up playing for Victor Mills, located in Greer just south of Greenville. Then, Lawrence Lollie Gray, who had played football for Clemson and was the organizer of the "Near Leaguers," a semiprofessional team, noticed Jackson enthusiastically pounding away with Black Betsy. Gray signed him up for his team. Some days Jackson played for that team; other days he performed for Victor Mills.

At that time, Joe was obsessed with the two passions of his life: baseball and Katie Wynn. The two teenagers spent many soft southern evenings talking of the future: of their getting married and of Joe's dream of a career in the booming sport of professional baseball.

Faced with no challenge from any other sports, delighted at rising attendance, and averaging nearly seven million fans a season, baseball was truly king of the hill. In the early 1900s there were 400 leagues in Chicago alone. All over the south, hundreds of semiprofessional and professional "barnstorming" teams traveled about offering challenges to local teams. Communities vied with each for the right to have a professional team represent them. For several years, Greenville civic leaders had labored to obtain one. So it was a matter of much pride when Greenville officials announced that their city would have a baseball franchise in the new Class D Carolina Association when the 1908 season got under way.

The New York Times had reported in 1900, "Rowdyism by the players on the field, syndicalism among the club owners, poor umpiring and talk of rival organizations . . . are the principal reasons for baseball's decline." But the report flew in the face of the reality that baseball in that America was all the rage. The game had only to be seen to be loved, a writer of the time noted. Other writers like Grantland Rice, Ring Lardner, and Hugh Fullerton romanticized and publicized the sport and the players who had names like Babe, Ping, Rube, Wahoo Sam, Mugsy, Chief, Muddy, Kid, Dummy, Hooks, Hod.

In 1900, the National League cut down from a dozen teams to eight: Boston, Brooklyn, Chicago, Cincinnati, New York, Philadelphia, Pittsburgh, and St. Louis. It was a pattern that would remain intact for fifty-three years—those eight teams of the National League whose names virtually every schoolboy was able to recite by heart. That year home plate became a 17-inch, 5-sided figure, replacing the 12-inch square.

On Opening Day of the new century the Philadelphia Phillies defeated the Boston Braves, 19–17, in ten innings, setting a record for most runs scored by two teams on the first day of the season. On October 20, 1900, the Cardinals withheld paying the final month's salary to all but five players, claiming that the team tied for fifth place because of gambling, late hours, and general dissipation.

In ballparks all over the country, Bull Durham signs decorated outfield fences. And those players lucky enough to bat a ball that hit the sign were rewarded with a fifty-dollar check by the tobacco company.

Fields of play were often oddly shaped and erratic. Many times outfield walls were formed by the contours of fans standing shoulder to shoulder. On June 9, 1901, 17,000 fans jammed in to watch a game in Cincinnati. The overflow crowd ringed the outfield and crowded close behind the infield. There were so many ground-rule doubles hit in that game that it was finally declared a forfeit.

Those who were unable to see the games at major league ballparks congregated at the local general stores of small towns and for a dime or fifteen cents listened to an operator recreate the play-by-play that came in on a telegraph wire. Baseball matinees, they were called, and those who listened reacted with cheers and jeers just as if they were at the actual game.

When catcher Roger Bresnahan began the practice of wearing shin guards in the early 1900s, grumblings came from the *New York Sun:* "The latest protection for catchers looks rather clumsy, besides delaying a game while the guards are strapped behind the knee and around the ankle, and it is doubtful if the fad will ever become popular."

In 1903, the American League gained recognition as a major circuit, banding together with the National League and the minor leagues into a framework called "Organized Baseball" under the supervision and jurisdiction of the National Commission. In mid-August of 1903 president Ban Johnson ordered all gambling and betting to cease at American League parks. No one paid any attention to his orders.

With their teams headed towards pennants, Pittsburgh's Barney Dreyfuss and Boston's Henry Killilea agreed to have their teams play a best-of-nine playoff after the season ended for the "Championship of the United States."

> The minimum price of admission shall be 50 cents and the visiting club shall be settled with by being paid 25 cents for every ticket sold.
>
> —World Series contract

The first World Series game was played at Boston's Huntington Street Park on October 1, 1903. The Pirates, who had won their third straight National League pennant and were one of the original franchises dating back to 1876, won the game 7–3, to the dismay of the hometown fans. Boston had entered the American League in 1901. The team was called the Americans, then the Somersets, then the Pilgrims. They became the Red Sox in 1907 because their owner's son John Taylor liked the color of the stockings the players wore. Pirate fans had earthier names for the Boston players who defeated them in the World Series. It was a victory that gave the American League a sense of legitimacy.

Throughout baseball's brief history, umpires had generally used long-handled brooms to dust off home plate and then discarded the brooms. But in 1904, outfielder Jack McCarthy of the Cubs hurt his ankle when he accidentally stepped on a broom trying to score from third base. League officials ordered all umpires to switch to a whisk broom, which they were to keep at the ready in their back pocket. That 1904, season Orator Jim O'Rourke, who had recorded the first hit in National League history, was employed as a catcher by McGraw. At age fifty-two O'Rourke became the oldest man in National League history to get a hit.

There was no World Series in 1904 because John McGraw's New York Giants refused to play against Boston, the American League repeat champion.

JOHN McGRAW: "Why should we play this upstart club or any other American League team for any postseason championship? We are champions of the only real major league."

McGraw's boycott was motivated by his anger at the American League for placing the Highlanders franchise in New York to compete against the Giants for fans. McGraw also harbored hostility towards Ban Johnson for what he called "unjust treatment" during his American League days as a member of the Baltimore Orioles.

By 1905, McGraw's ruffled feelings had been smoothed. The World Series resumed. New York's Christy Mathewson pitched three shutouts against the Philadelphia Athletics, and McGraw's Giants took the title in five games. The Series was an economic shot in the arm for baseball, and an image-enhancing moment for John J. McGraw, the man they called "Mugsy."

Young Joe Jackson, playing in a Textile League game, also had an image-enhancing moment. He was fortunate that a writer from the local newspaper and a scout from the newly formed Greenville Spinners saw it. The hyperbolic newspaper report recalled the moment: "In the final inning with three on and two out Joe cracked the horse hide a swat that carried it into the next township and won the game."

After the game the scout signed Jackson to a $75-a-month contract. Joe Jackson began his professional career, playing under manager Tommy Stouch for the Greenville Spinners in 1908. In his first game, an exhibition contest against the Boston Nationals, he homered, tripled, and doubled. Stouch announced that when the season began, Jackson, the only ex-millhand on a Spinner team composed primarily of middle-class youths from various states, would bat third in the batting order and play center field.

With the beginnings of a career in professional baseball seemingly secured, Joe Jackson and Katie set a marriage date: July 19, an off day for the Spinners.

The 1908 official Opening Day game saw Greenville pitted against the Anderson Electricians. Grandstand seats were 40 cents. Bleachers seats cost two bits. And the left-field foul line was crowded with cars, buggies, and carriages, all at 50 cents per vehicle. Black fans sat in the restricted colored section and cheered on the Spinners, who wore ice-cream-white home uniforms.

It was a wonderful day for the home team—a 14–1 victory. And it was a wonderful day for Joe Jackson—two doubles and a triple and a dazzling, grasping catch that got the fans on their feet. That was how he began in pro ball, a nineteen-year-old in the full bloom of his talent.

As the Carolina season moved into the middle of May, there was little doubt in the minds of all who saw him that Joe Jackson was the most outstanding player in the league. Batting .350, hitting home runs, and making big plays in the field, he was a natural.

Joe was recommended by a writer friend to Joe Cantillon, former manager of the Washington Senators, who came down to check out the phenom. But Cantillon was not impressed.

JOE CANTILLON: "He's simply a bush leaguer flash in the pan and will prove a farce in the big leagues."

But Tommy Stouch knew what he had. As the story goes, he called his friend Connie Mack, owner of the Philadelphia Athletics, and told him about all "this natural talent." Mack dispatched injured A's outfielder Socks Seybold to check out Jackson and his Spinner teammate Hyder Barr in a game the Spinners played against the Charlotte Hornets. A double, a triple, and a home run by Jackson. Seybold was sold.

Another version of the Joe Jackson discovery comes from Connie Mack himself: "An apothecary down in that burg who had previously written me some good tips in regard to young prospects kept urging me to give this fellow a trial. But what intrigues me most was that this prodigy played without shoes. 'He doesn't wear spikes or in fact any kind of covering for his feet,' came the tip. He's so fast that he can tear around those bases without any such help. They call him 'Shoeless Joe.' "

They did call him "Shoeless Joe," and he became a baseball myth, a mix of fact and fantasy.

One oft-repeated account has him playing in the outfield sans shoes amid the debris of stubble, glass, and rocks.

"I'm quittin'," he supposedly told Tommy Stouch.

"Are the rocks and glass cutting your feet?"

"Naw. But they're fuzzin' up the ball and I can't throw it."

Another account comes from Carter "Scoop" Latimer, former sports editor for the *Greenville News*. In Anderson, South Carolina, according to Latimer, Jackson was called in from the outfield to pitch a game. The next day Jackson was back in the outfield nursing a very sore foot. When his time came to bat, he slipped off his shoe and stepped into the batter's box. He then slammed a home run. "As he rounded third base, a fan shouted out 'You shoeless son of a bitch!' " said Latimer. "As a cub reporter free-lancing for a Greenville paper I picked it up and tagged him Shoeless Joe, and the nick-name stuck."

Then there is the October 1949 *Sport* magazine account by Jackson of how he was tagged with the "Shoeless Joe" nickname.

JOE JACKSON: "We had only twelve men on the roster. I was first off a pitcher, but when I wasn't pitching I played in the outfield. I played in a brand new pair of shoes one day and they wore blisters on my feet. The next day we came up short of players, a couple of men hurt and one missing. Tommy Stouch, the manager, told me I'd just have to play, blisters or not.

"I tried it with my old shoes on and just couldn't make it. He told me I'd have to play anyway, so I threw away the shoes and went to the outfield in my stockinged feet. I hadn't put out much until the seventh inning. I hit a long triple and I turned it on. The bleachers were close to the baselines there. As I pulled into third some big guy stood up and hollered.

" 'You shoeless sonofagun you!'

"They picked it up and started calling me Shoeless Joe all around the league, and it stuck. I never played the outfield barefoot, and that was the only day I ever played in my stockinged feet, but it stuck with me."

A person who would stick with Joe Jackson through the high moments and the low became his bride on Sunday, the nineteenth of July, 1908; the nineteen-year-old star of the Carolina Association married fifteen-year-old Katherine Wynn. The *Greenville News* reported the event: "Joe Jackson made the greatest home-run of his career on Sunday. The home-run was made on Cupid's diamond and the victory was a fair young lady."

On August 22, the Philadelphia Athletics announced that they had purchased Joe Jackson's contract from the Spinners for $325. He was expected to report to Philadelphia after the Carolina Association season ended.

That same day two of the most exciting major league pennant races in baseball history played out. The New York Giants and the Chicago Cubs went head-to-head in the National League. In Chicago and New York electric bulletin boards with electric diamonds chronicled the race. At the Gotham Theater and at Madison Square Garden in New York City hundreds lined up to watch "Compton's Baseball Bulletin," described in newspapers as "a wonder of its time."

Chicago would win the pennant on the basis of what would forever be known as "the bonehead play"—Giant player Fred Merkle's failure to touch second base on what should have been the game-winning hit. The Giants and the Pirates would tie for second place, a game off the pace. In the American League, Detroit, Cleveland, and Chicago battled through the humid heat of August. The Tigers would win the pennant on the last day of the season with a bare .004 margin of victory over Cleveland.

Those northern cities were lit up by the exciting pennant races, and Greenville was aglow over the batting exploits of its native son. In its first year of operation, its fledgling franchise had produced a batting champion. Joe Jackson had hit for a .346 average to lead the Carolina Association.

His time of celebration was brief, for a couple of days after the season ended, Jackson was a reluctant passenger on a train headed north to Philadelphia to report to the Athletics. Hyder Barr was with him and so was Tommy Stouch, as part guide, part nursemaid, part jailer. Stouch listened patiently as Jackson drawled out his misgivings and uncertainties, his fears about big-city life and city slickers. As the train moved north, Jackson's complaints grew. Three times he managed to slip away from Stouch only to be rounded up and re-routed north.

CONNIE MACK: "He was the town hero on the mill team and thoroughly satisfied with his lot. He was the center of attraction at the village store in the evening and the whole town rang with his exploits. The trouble was that Jackson didn't want to come to the big leagues."

2

Philadelphia

Philadelphia was a new world for Joseph Jefferson Jackson. It was also a new world for thousands upon thousands of immigrants who arrived from southern and eastern Europe. Jews, Russians, Poles, Irish, and Italians, jammed into booming and crowded old cities like Philadelphia. Baseball, a game without a clock, was a way to escape the shrillness of factory whistles and time-clock punching, and immigrants flocked to it as they assimilated into the culture and learned the ceremonies of America.

The new world of major league baseball that Jackson entered was one of the "dead ball," high batting averages, low earned runs averages, big hit totals, and small run totals. Pitchings was dominant.

Prior to 1906, home teams supplied baseballs. Many were frozen, scuffed, or scraped. Numerous complaints resulted in switching the responsibility and control of supplying balls to the umpires. Directed by owners, umpires attempted to ration the use of baseballs to two or three a game. Fans were required to return balls hit into the stands. After just a couple of innings of use the baseballs became softer, sometimes lopsided and speckled with the stains of licorice, dirt, grass, tobacco juice, and any other substances pitchers had the nerve and imagination to apply.

Overmatched as they were against hurlers and oft-invisible trick pitches, batters compensated with nuance and guile.

Games were rarely decided on a single swing but on the cumulative efforts of teams working together—the parts creating the whole. Bunting, sacrificing, and placement of the ball were fashioned into art forms by players like Ty Cobb, Nap Lajoie, Willie Keeler, Honus Wagner, and other legends.

Joe Jackson's new world was one where first-class hotels were off limits to ballplayers, where waiters used the code words "baseball steaks" for poor-quality meat, where superstition, cussing, crashing, and crass pranks characterized the behavior of players.

In 1908, as Jackson entered the major leagues, owners had agreed to a new rule change. A batter was credited with a sacrifice fly and not a time at bat if the runner scored on a fly ball that was caught. 1908 was the final major league season of nineteenth-century throwback "Iron Man" Joe McGinnity, who pitched both games of a doubleheader a record five times in his career. A remarkable physical specimen, McGinnity would continue to pitch in the minor leagues and finally end his career at age fifty-four.

For the Athletics of Philadelphia, 1908 was a rebuilding season. The team would play its final season in Columbia Park and wind up in sixth place, twenty-two games behind the pennant-winning Tigers.

The look of the country was flush on the 6'2", 180-pound Jackson, whose coal black hair was parted in the middle and flattened down. He gathered himself together and stepped off the train in Philadelphia along with Hyder Barr. Dizzied by the swirling crowds of people, the fast movement, and the bigness of it all, Jackson and Barr checked their bags at the station and reported to Columbia Park at 29th Street and Columbia Avenue in Brewerytown, the famed beer-producing section of Philadelphia.

Just twenty years old, homesick, and totally out of his element, Jackson was a stark counterpoint to another twenty-year-old baseball player of that time, a pitcher for the Washington Senators named Walter Johnson. On September 7, 1908, Johnson would shut out the New York Highlanders for the third time in a four-game Labor Day series played in New York City.

The enormous press buildup that Jackson had received was something that Philadelphia had not experienced for many years. All around the city baseball fans talked about the new kid from the Carolinas.

Jackson played center field and batted cleanup in the first game he played. Columbia Park seated almost 15,000, but only 3,000 fans were there on August 25, 1908, a dank day. One can only wonder what Joe Jackson thought, being in a major league ballpark for the first time. Did he smell the aroma of barley, hops, and malt that wafted in the air from the breweries located close by the little ballpark as he stepped into the batter's box with two outs and two on base for the first of his 4,981 major league at bats? The crowd rose to cheer him.

In 1908, the rule that banned discoloring of the baseball by rubbing it with soil was in effect. But there was no ban on the spitball, and that was the specialty of Heinie Berger, Cleveland's pitcher that day, who was on the way to a 13–8 record.

Berger looked in for the sign and delivered the ball to Jackson out of an exaggerated windup. Jackson sliced the ball down the right-field line. It went foul. But he measured the next pitch carefully with his eyes and bat and lined the ball to left for the first of his 1,774 hits, and the first of his 785 runs batted in. An over-the-shoulder catch, a throw from the fence in left center field that was nearly 400 feet, and some fine baserunning— Joe Jackson showed off the whole package that August day in Philadelphia.

CONNIE MACK: "If nothing happens to him, he should develop rapidly into one of the greatest players the game has yet produced. But give the boy time to learn and develop and don't expect too much of him from the start. Remember he is only a boy and this is his first year out."

That night, Barr, well known as a ladies' man, took up with a girl. He convinced Jackson to go back to the train station alone to recover both their bags. At the station Jackson heard the announcer call out: "Baltimore, Washington, Richmond, Danville, Greensboro, Charlotte, Spartanburgh, Greenville,

Anderson. . . .'' The words sent Jackson to the window, where he purchased a ticket for Greenville. But club officials, already aware of the rookie's previous aborted attempts at flight, felt that Joe Jackson and a railroad station were nothing but trouble. They were right. They rushed down to the depot and were able to round him up just before his train came in.

JOE JACKSON: "It wasn't anything I had against Mr. Mack or the ball club. Mr. Mack was a mighty fine man, and he taught me more baseball than any other manager I had. I just didn't like Philadelphia.''

It was not only Philadelphia. It was a lot of the players on the Athletics.

CONNIE MACK: "My other players didn't know what to make of him. He was a regular sphinx, never entered into conversation with anyone.''

The Tigers came to Philadelphia for a four-game series. The first two games were rained out. With time on their hands and no games to report on, the Philly writers devoted much space to what they said was going to be a great individual baseball rivalry—the new star in town, Joseph Jackson, and the four-year pro Ty Cobb, who was on his way to winning his second of a dozen American League batting titles.

Some of the Athletics resented the extensive press coverage given to Jackson. Moreover, they were turned off by his dour demeanor and obvious illiteracy. Alternately ignoring and abusing him, they seemed to delight in playing practical jokes at his expense. Perhaps the lowest prank they devised was tricking the young player into drinking from a finger bowl after dinner.

Fed up and feeling foolish and out of place, Jackson once again made his way to the train station. This time he managed to board the train back to Greenville.

CONNIE MACK: "He packed his old fashioned 'war bag' and hit the rattlers for home. I think the big city and the big crowds scared him. I found out later that he was in love with a Greenville belle and couldn't stand for the separation.''

Newspaper reports of Jackson's absence attributed it to fear of a head-to-head confrontation with Ty Cobb. His mother denied such reports and claimed he'd returned home to be with his wife, who was ill, and to pay a final visit to an uncle who was not expected to live. "Joe is game and has always been game," the robust matriarch said.

The Athletics and Tigers played two doubleheaders to make up for the earlier rainouts. Cobb managed just one hit in fourteen at bats in those games. Perhaps he had Joe Jackson on his mind. For ten days Joe remained in Greenvile. There was no public comment. It seemed that his major league career would be concluded after one game because there was talk in the newspapers that Connie Mack was planning on having him blacklisted from major league baseball if he did not return to Philadelphia.

On September 7 he returned, played in four more games, and fumed in silence all the time at the continuing abuse dumped on him by some of his Philadelphia teammates. Finally, unable to take any more, the humbled and homesick rookie once again hopped a train and returned to South Carolina. Mack suspended him.

In five games Jackson had batted just .177. Joe Cantillon's prophesy that he was just a busher and would prove a farce in the big leagues seemed to be coming true.

The patriarchal Connie Mack offered to get a teacher to work with Joe during the off season so he could learn his ABCs. But Jackson refused. "It don't take no school stuff to help a fella play ball," he said.

Instead, during the off-season he worked in the butcher shop that he had helped his father purchase. The oldest child and the favorite of his mother, he spent a lot of time helping her with the household chores, peeling apples and baking bread.

CONNIE MACK: "I sent Socks Seybold down after him the following spring. It took two days of earnest argument before Socks could induce him to make a try for the big league again."

In the spring of 1909, Jackson wrapped Black Betsy up carefully in a long piece of white cotton cloth and reported to

Atlanta, where the spring training camp of the rebuilding Philadelphia Athletics was located.

The sportswriters around Philadelphia dubbed the bright young players on the Athletics "Yannigans," a term for rookies that had been in use for several years. The group consisted of Joe Jackson, Stuffy McInnis, Amos Strunk, Eddie Collins, Home Run Baker. As the Athletics barnstormed north, it was plain to all that the confident and capable Yannigans, especially Jackson, were much more than a match for the veteran players.

CONNIE MACK: "He made the headlines in Montgomery and New Orleans, but this didn't mean anything to him because praise and censure was all the same to him. He never knew what was in the papers because he couldn't read. At Louisville, he hit a ball over the right-field fence, one of the longest homers ever hit in that neck of the woods. He became an overnight sensation . . . but he did not want to go to Philadelphia. . . . I had him under the escort of the entire team as we headed north."

The train carrying the Athletics stopped at Reading, Pennsylvania. On the opposite railroad siding, more than fifty large milk cans stood in a row all with red destination labels. Jackson stared at the milk cans, transfixed by the sight.

Jackson turned to Mack. "I wish that you'd put a red tag on me and ship me along with the milk cans down south."

"Where would you like to go?"

"Savannah."

On March 28, Connie Mack optioned Joe Jackson to Savannah in the South Atlantic League.

In 1909, the United States was a nation of 90 million people. Electric streetcars, trolleys, had made ballparks much more accessible for fans. Railroad systems linked city to city and made it possible for teams to play opponents over a wider geographical region. On baseball's Opening Day, President William Howard Taft threw out the first ball, beginning what would become an American tradition.

WILLIAM HOWARD TAFT: "The game of baseball is a clean,

straight game and it summons to its presence everybody who enjoys clean straight athletics."

It is ironic that Taft, one of the least athletic presidents of the United States, established this precedent while Theodore Roosevelt, who was one of the most athletic presidents, disdained what would become the American pastime.

ALICE ROOSEVELT LONGWORTH: "Father and all of us regarded baseball as a molly-coddle game. Tennis, football, lacrosse, boxing, polo, yes. They are violent, which appealed to us. But baseball? Father wouldn't watch it, not even at Harvard."

The Athletics in 1909 moved into brand-new Shibe Park at 21st Street and Lehigh, baseball's first steel-and-concrete ballpark. The sod was transplanted from Columbia Park. Named for Athletics majority stockholder Ben Shibe of the baseball manufacturing firm of A.J. Reach, the park would be the home of the Athletics for forty-five years and a lucky charm for Connie Mack, who would win four pennants and three world championships in his first six years there. An almost churchlike French Renaissance dome, where Connie Mack's office was located, topped the exterior roof behind home plate. One especially modern feature was the installation of water plugs in the stands of the single-decked facility. They were there in case of fire and to expedite hosing down and cleaning. Colorful six-foot-tall signs advertised products such as "Regal Shoes" and "White Rock" on the outfield walls. A ladder in front of the left-field scoreboard went all the way to the top. It was 360 feet down the lines, 515 feet to the center-field fence, and almost 400 feet in the power alleys—all custom-ordered by Mack to accommodate the needs of his team. The pitcher's mound was twenty inches high—also especially designed for the Athletics. Later that season, when landlords rented space to fans on the rooftops of buildings adjacent to the ballpark, Connie Mack ordered the stadium wall raised.

Opening Day at Shibe Park was April 12, 1909. Vendors arrived early and sold lemonade, popcorn, peanuts, and A's pennants. A huge crowd of 30,000 came out, mostly men sporting derby hats and wearing suits and ties. There were seats available for only 20,000; the other 10,000 purchased standing-room-only tickets. Most of them congregated in the outfield behind ropes. As late as 1900 some clubs allowed fans to park their automobiles or carriages in the outfield, although the practice had since been discontinued. But there was such a collection of horses and buggies parked outside of Shibe Park for the 3:15 game that the scene resembled a cavalry camp.

Throughout the world of major league baseball there was change that 1909 season. Several new rules were in place. One credited a catcher with a putout on a bunt on a third strike. Another took away credit to a runner for a stolen base on an attempted double steal if either runner was thrown. The New York Highlanders were called "Yankees" by headline writers in newspapers for the first time in 1909. The name would prove popular with fans. It would also be a blessing for layout editors who had struggled for years to squeeze the eleven-letter word "Highlanders" into headlines.

Down in Savannah, Joe Jackson delighted in his new surroundings. He was in his element: down-home cooking, freedom from taunting teammates, enjoying the friendship and encouragement of manager Bobby Gilks. It all proved a tonic for him. Jackson rapped out thirty-six hits in his first eighty at bats for a .450 average.

One moment in that season in the South Atlantic League is part of the stuff that made Joe Jackson a legend. Savannah played Chattanooga. Going into the top of the ninth inning, the Tennessee pitcher, Prince Gaskill, had given up but just one hit and led 1–0. He walked the Savannah leadoff batter in the ninth, and that brought Jackson to the plate. Bobby Gilks walked out from the bench in his civilian clothes and told Jackson, "Swing away. Kill it."

The first pitch came in and Jackson slugged the ball over the right-field fence.

Everything was going well for Jackson, but the same could not be said for Savannah. With the team losing, Gilks paid the price of failure. He was fired.

Although Jackson did not talk about how much he missed Gilks, his body language expressed his feelings. His mopey demeanor and sluggish movements on the field underscored a dropping batting average. When the season finally came to an end, his average had dropped almost a hundred points from his season high. Yet Jackson still managed to wind up batting .354 in 136 games. That made it two minor league seasons for Jackson and two batting titles.

On September 4, 1909, the man the newspapers called "Home Run Joe" and "Stonewall" rejoined the A's. The previous year when Jackson was originally called up by Philadelphia, the team was just playing out the string. This time it was different. The emerging Athletics were in the midst of a tough pennant race in second place behind the Tigers.

CONNIE MACK: "We brought him and his missus up. We tried to teach them our way of doing things, but it still was difficult for them to get adjusted. Our players played pranks on Joe, and he regarded them with suspicion."

Jackson's first major league appearance in 1909 was against New York.

JOE JACKSON: "I hit the first pitch Jack Warhop threw me for a double. I had a single later and had two for three."

The box score of the time does not confirm Jackson's memory. In all, he played in just five games for the 1909 Athletics, managing five hits in seventeen at bats. And then he went back home to South Carolina, fretting about the limited opportunity he had been given.

That year the new National League President was Thomas Lynch. He succeeded Harry Pulliam, who had committed suicide the previous summer. In 1910, the rubber-centered baseball was replaced by one with a cork middle for "occasional" play. Then the ball was given a thinner leather cover and yarn that was more tightly wound and had less protrusion to the seams. All of this made the baseball more resilient than it had been, thus generating more offense, however sparingly.

On April 20, Addie Joss of Cleveland pitched the second no-hitter of his career, beating Chicago 1–0. On May 4, 1910, both the Browns and Cardinals played home games in St. Louis. President Taft, always the polite politician, saw parts of both games at Robison Field and Sportsman's Park and grumbled a bit about the lack of power and slugging exhibited in major league games. The White Sox that season would personify what Taft was talking about, as they posted the lowest team batting average in baseball history. Their seven home runs as a team were also a record low. The other Chicago team, the Cubs, would win their fourth championship in five years, and F.P. Adams in the *New York Mail* would publish his Tinker-to-Evers-to-Chance refrain.

Player salaries averaged about $2,500 by 1910, with some superstars receiving as much as $12,000. At the end of the pay scale, though, were those who made just a thousand dollars a season.

The rebuilt Athletics began their domination of baseball of that time—a string of winning four pennants in five years. They had star pitchers like Jack Coombs, Chief Bender, and Eddie Plank. Their $100,000 infield consisted of Stuffy McInnis at first base, Eddie Collins at second base, Frank "Home Run" Baker at third base, and Jack Barry at shortstop. With players such as these available to Connie Mack, Joe Jackson was the odd man out.

The roster of the Athletics showed Mack's touch in being able to match a player with the right position. It also reflected his preference for college-educated players.

CONNIE MACK: "These boys, who knew their Greek and Latin and their algebra and geometry and trigonometry, put intelligence into the game."

The 1910 Athletics were probably the most highly educated team in history to that point: Eddie Collins of Columbia University, Jack Barry of Holy Cross, Jack Coombs of Colby, and Eddie Plank of Gettysburg. "Connie Mack's college boys," they were called.

The former millhand on the team, the only illiterate, sullen, and out-of-place ballplayer, Jackson posed a problem for Mack. He did not want to trade the young ballplayer, yet he couldn't seem to fit him into the dynasty he was carefully building. So the manager they dubbed the "Grand Old Man," sometimes shortened to GOM, simply assigned Jackson in 1910 to the minors once again—this time to the New Orleans Pelicans of the Southern League.

The Pelicans had a close working relationship with the Cleveland Naps, and played several spring training games against the major league team. Throughout that spring, as Jackson unleashed Black Betsy against the Naps, Cleveland owner Charles Somers looked on in envy. He then made a decision that would affect the direction of young Jackson's life.

The big Opening Day headline in the major leagues was Walter Johnson's shutting down the Athletics on one hit. "The Big Train" was off in high gear. But so was Joe Jackson. There was an electronic scoreboard in the New Orleans ballpark, and it lit up time after time like a pinball machine as it recorded Jackson's batting pyrotechnics. After fifteen games as a member of the Pelicans, he was batting over .500.

New Orleans was a cosmopolitan city with many different nationalities, friendly fans, and supportive media—all of which buttressed Jackson's sense of security and well being. He even developed some enduring friendships with opposing players. One of them was outfielder Joe Phillips of the Mobile Sea Gulls. The proprietor of a vaudeville house in his West Virginia home town during the offseason, Phillips introduced Jackson to the world of show business. The two frequented vaudeville establishments all over New Orleans, and Phillips explained that someday Joe could make good money as a famous baseball star plying his wares on the vaudeville circuit.

When the Southern League season came to a close, a pattern repeated itself for the third straight year. Joe Jackson had amazed everyone with his fielding heroics game after game. He had been selected to another league All Star team. He had batted .354 and won another minor league batting title. And once again, he grudgingly boarded a train for the trip north to a major league team.

Only this time Jackson, along with his wife Katie, was

headed not to Philadelphia but to Cleveland. Connie Mack had traded Jackson to Cleveland for a reported $325 and outfielder Bristol Robotham Lord, better known as Bris Lord, whose nickname was "the Human Eyeball."

CONNIE MACK: "I knew exactly what I was doing. Bristol Lord, of course, helped me at the time. Jackson was a rather difficult man to handle. I knew our players didn't like Jackson, but that isn't why I traded him. I also knew Joe had great possibilities as a hitter. At that time things were going none too well for Charlie Somers in Cleveland, and I was anxious to do him a good turn in appreciation for the way he had helped us out in Philadelphia in the early days of the league. So I let him have Jackson."

3

Cleveland

In mid-September Joe Jackson arrived in Cleveland, a city with a population of almost 600,000, making it the sixth-largest in America. Back in 1890, only about a third of the nation's population lived in a city or town. But driven by the isolation of rural life and the dream of what the city had to offer, more and more people began flocking to urban centers. Immigrants also steamed into metropolitan areas; by 1910, cities accounted for nearly half the nation's population. The growth of the city and the rise of professional baseball were concurrent.

The original 1869 nickname of the Cleveland baseball team was the Forest Citys, because of the city's many trees. Two decades later the name was changed to Spiders. In 1900, the team was called the Cleveland Blues because its players wore bright blue uniforms. By 1903, the nickname once again changed—this time to the Naps, in honor of one of their stars, Larry Napoleon Lajoie.

Lajoie, in 1910, was Cleveland's main man, a thirteen-year American League star. But Ohio newspapers were all agog over the new man who in three years in the minor leagues had won three batting titles. They called him "the Champion Batter of Dixie," the "Southern Star," and the "Carolina Crashsmith."

Joe Jackson reported to manager Deacon McGuire in the home-team clubhouse located beneath the stands on the first-base side of League Park. He was given a loose-fitting white home uniform—with a "C" in blue on the left shirt sleeve and a smaller "C" on the little baseball cap—a pair of blue knee-length heavy woolen socks, and baggy pants that were held up by a black leather belt. Penciled in to bat third in the lineup, Jackson was positioned in center field.

In his first at bat for Cleveland, Jackson crushed the ball—one of his patented, hard, low line drive, "blue darters." The ball shot at the second baseman, who threw up his little glove in self-defense. But the force of the ball ripped the glove off the player and knocked him down.

Newspapers in New Orleans, Savannah, and Greenville kept their readers informed of their local hero's accomplishments:

JACKSON DRIVES BALL TO THE TALL AND UNCUT—LONGEST HIT EVER RECORDED IN CLEVELAND
GREENVILLE BOY MAKING GOOD

In a game against his former Philadelphia teammates, Jackson put on a show. Eddie Collins, with one out and a runner on third base, hit a deep drive to Jackson. As he gloved the ball, Jackson saw the runner tagging up at third base trying to score. Jackson braced himself and fired the ball home on a line into the catcher's mitt for a double play.

Against Washington on September 17, Jackson came to bat in the eighth inning against right-hander Bob Groom. He got all of the pitch and slugged it to deep center for a home run. It was one of the longest homers hit by anyone that season, and the first of Joe Jackson's 54 major league career home runs.

In twenty games for Cleveland at the tail end of that 1910 season, Joe Jackson batted .387. But one can only wonder what went through his mind as he watched the scrambling intrigue for the batting title play out between teammate Nap Lajoie and Ty Cobb.

It was on April 25, 1901, that Lajoie had played in his first game in the newly formed American League for the Philadelphia Athletics and rapped out three hits on the way to a .422

season batting average and the Triple Crown. Less than a month later, Lajoie came to bat against the White Sox with the bases loaded. He was walked intentionally, in one of the rarest of managerial moves.

Now, with two games left in the 1910 season, Ty Cobb decided to bench himself rather than run the risk of losing the batting title to Lajoie.

The season came down to the last day, October 9. Lajoie needed eight hits to win the batting championship and the Chalmers Award, named for the Chalmers Motor Company. In a doubleheader against St. Louis, he recorded eight hits in eight at bats. Only one of the hits was of the outfield variety—a triple banged over the head of the center fielder. Newspapers called the other seven hits "suspect" bunt singles down the third-base line. They were more than suspect. Red Corriden, the Browns' rookie third baseman, was under explicit orders from his manager, "Peach Pie" Jack O'Connor, to play very deep and encourage the bunt. O'Connor also bribed and bullied the official scorer, offering a forty-dollar new suit of clothes as barter for bunts scored as hits. The scorer followed the suggestion so zealously that he even credited Lajoie with a hit on a play by the St. Louis shortstop that was an obvious throwing error to first base.

The finagling was still not done. Hugh Fullerton was yet to be heard from. "Fair is fair," said the popular and widely respected baseball writer. He announced his reversal of a ruling he had made earlier that season as an official scorer when he had ruled that Ty Cobb had reached base on an error. Now retreating, he said Cobb, after the fact, should be credited with a hit.

When all the fussing and finagling was done, the final averages were Ty Cobb, .3850687; Napoleon Lajoie, .3840947.

A *Chicago Tribune* poem of the time underscored the entire mess and proved to be a harbinger of things to come:

When Larry [Lajoie] faced the St. Louis five
He'd eight to go to be secure.

And what they thought he might require
They slipped it to him, that's pretty sure.

What must a meek outsider think
When tricks like that they put across?
When at one frameup they will wink
How do we know what games they will toss?

The whole episode was investigated by American League president Ban Johnson. Clearing all parties, he decided that Cobb was the batting champion. Then, as balm and whitewash for the whole matter, he exerted his influence and arranged with the Chalmers Motor Company for both Cobb and Lajoie to be awarded brand-new cars.

Despite Ban Johnson's good feelings about the Cobb-Lajoie fiasco, Browns president Hedges did not hedge his. On October 15, just before the World Series between the Chicago Cubs, who had won their fourth National League pennant in five years, and Connie Mack's young Philadelphia Athletics, who had won a league-record 102 games, he fired manager Jack O'Connor for his role in what he termed the "Lajoie travesty."

Lost in the shuffle of what some writers called "the Battle of the Auto Chasers" was the fact that Jackson's batting average was higher than either Cobb's or Lajoie's, higher than anyone's in the American League. Unfortunately, Jackson didn't have nearly enough at bats to qualify for the batting title.

Cleveland owner Charley Somers, along with Ban Johnson and Charles Comiskey, was a key figure in the founding of the American League. Somers developed a fondness for Jackson. He also was very impressed with the young player's accomplishments.

"You're the greatest natural hitter I ever saw," Somers told him. "Some day you're going to be the finest player in all of baseball. But you need more than that. You need an education. Now that the season is over I'll send you to school. It will do a lot for you. Between now and next spring you'll be a different man."

It was the same sort of suggestion proferred by Connie Mack, and Jackson gave the same sort of reply. He agreed with Somers and thanked him for his kind words.

"But I won't be satisfied around a book," Jackson said. "None o' my people ever had schoolin' anyway. I ain't afraid to tell the world that it don't take school stuff to help a fella play ball."

So Jackson returned home to South Carolina after the 1910 season, to the laid-back style of life, to old overalls and home cooking. He ate well but never overate. Throughout his career his playing weight of 186 pounds rarely varied more than a pound.

When neighbors and friends came around to visit with him, they delighted in hearing all the fabulous stories of the big city, the tales of the sounds of the tin lizzies chugging up and down the streets and avenues, the clanging trolleys with their posters featuring baseball personalities like John McGraw, who endorsed Tuxedo tobacco this way: "Tuxedo gives to my pipe smoking a keen enjoyment that I have experienced with no other tobacco."

All of this was fascinating news, but what the neighbors and friends enjoyed hearing about most were the inside stories about their favorite major league players.

Their favorite of favorites, of course, was Joe Jackson. And he brought a flush to the cheeks of many when he told them that after what he had done in 1910, he thought he had a good chance to win the 1911 batting title.

Katie was always there, as childhood sweetheart, wife, contract reader, business manager, and tutor. She spent many hours schooling her husband in signing his paychecks. He painfully practiced copying her writing of his name, but to him it was no more than an abstract design. Now, in the offseason of 1910, she became involved behind the scenes helping her husband in contract negotiations with Somers.

JOE JACKSON: "He wasn't thinking of giving me more than $4,000, and he wouldn't listen to me. But we did some horse trading. I told Mr. Somers that if I hit .400 he should give me the $10,000, and that if I don't you don't give me a cent. We struck a deal."

Spurred by the financial incentive of the "deal," Jackson departed early from his home in Brandon for spring training, which he began with the Pelicans in New Orleans. Newspapers there called him the most popular player in the city's history. Surprisingly, some of the northern newspapers featured negative stories about him. A few claimed that he pulled away from the plate; others revived the old Ty Cobb fiasco from his Philadelphia days and labeled Jackson a coward. Jackson supporters scoffed at these reports. They claimed it was just that newspaper fellows had to find something to write about. Others thought there was a hidden agenda to them—Jackson's illiteracy. Of course Jackson was unable to read any of this, but when Katie and others told him what some reporters had written, he responded, "We'll see about that."

Finishing up with the Pelicans, Jackson joined the Naps in Alexandria, Louisiana, for a continuation of his spring training. When he arrived in camp, he looked very different from the roughly dressed rookie of a year before. Now he sported double-breasted suits and a felt hat of the porkpie style popular at the time. Most writers liked him and his easygoing ways, but there was one journalist who disliked him from the start.

HUGH FULLERTON: "A man who can't read or write simply can't meet the requirements of baseball as it is played today."

On April 12, 1911, President William Howard Taft threw out the first ball at the opening game of the Washington Senators and expressed hopes that the new cork-center baseball to be used in both leagues would stimulate offense. The President got his wish that season as National League offense increased by 500 runs; the American League doubled that figure.

Three days after Taft threw out the first ball, Walter Johnson, signed to a brand-new three-year contract at $7,000 a year, tied a major league record by striking out four batters in the fifth inning as Washington defeated Boston 1–0.

That season E.S. Barnard, the secretary of the Cleveland

team who would go on to be president of the American League, arranged for a sympathetic literate type to room with Joe Jackson. The roommate read letters aloud to him. Sometimes Jackson would pick out one of the letters he had received and make a big deal of reading it silently. Then he would give it to his roommate with the phrase: "Get this, the stuff is rich." The "rich" stuff usually was about the need for new netting wire on the chicken corral on the farm or information that taxes were due on this or that date.

A creature of habit, Jackson was also very superstitious. Black bats and hairpins were two of his fetishes. He would pick up every pin he could find, the rustier the better. There were times his pockets were literally bulging with them. When he got into a batting slump, he would claim the "charm" had worn off, dispose of all his pins, and start his collection again.

The Jacksons rented an apartment on Lexington Avenue close by League Park. Katie would settle in at every home game in her favorite perch, alone in a seat in the last row of the grandstand behind home plate. The Jacksons called it "the hunch," the superstition that her sitting there in that same seat game after game brought her husband good luck out on the playing field. She took her duties as "hunch" guardian, cheerleader, and scorekeeper seriously. However, her best efforts were reserved for the role of the devoted wife.

When the seventh inning came around, no matter the circumstances of the game, Katie left the ballpark and went back to the apartment to begin readying a home-cooked meal for Joe. It was a ritual practiced without interruption. Part of the reason was nutritional, but thrift was also a consideration, for Jackson was never a big spender, especially when he had no reason to be. He made it a practice to sew a $10 or $20 bill in the lining of his coat to be sure he had some cash available when he needed it.

League Park was the home of the Cleveland American League team. Situated at the eastern end of the city at the corner of East 66th Street and Lexington Avenue, it occupied a site selected by Cleveland owner F.D. Robinson. The Payne and Wade streetcars passed close by the main entrance to the park. Thus Robinson, who also owned the streetcar company, delighted in seeing his customers dropped off by one of his business enterprises. He was delighted even more to see them sauntering into the ballpark to patronize another one of his enterprises.

Between the 1909 and 1910 seasons, steel was used to reinforce and enlarge League Park. When Jackson joined Cleveland, the right-field fence had been remodeled with twenty feet of concrete and twenty feet of screen resting on top of that. Batters took aim at the wall just 290 feet from home plate, and there were those who were able to jerk balls over the fence into the street. Some of the baseballs struck nearby buildings, and each season the team was forced to pay out cash to replace at least a score of smashed windows.

For a right fielder playing the wall, it was a game of truth or consequences, an exercise in guessing: would the ball bounce true or in a crazy-quilt pattern off the wall? Would it fall dead to the base of the wall? Would it stick in the screen?

A game in vogue with the youth of Cleveland was "Wall." Using garage doors, brick walls, tin cans—whatever kind of surface they could hit with a ball—the kids would play the game, emulating the efforts of Joe Jackson.

They called him the "outfielding billiardist" because of his unique ability to play fly balls caroming off the right-field wall. He used his powerful arm to hold players to singles on shots that were sure doubles. And, as a hitter, he made his own billiard shots off the oddly constructed walls.

During batting practice, fans would cluster outside the right-field wall. They would wait for Joe Jackson and other outfielders to flip a ball over the fence. Then the scramble would begin. Free admission was given to anyone who brought a retrieved ball into the park. When the game began, a flock of kids and some adults listened for the sound of the bat hitting the ball, the clamor of the crowd, and the sight of the white sphere coming over that right-field fence.

On May 14, more than 15,000 fans came out to see Cleveland play its first Sunday game. They were rewarded as the home team romped 14–3 over New York. Ten days later Nap Lajoie, who was Jackson's best friend on the team, was side-lined by an abdominal ailment. He wound up playing in just ninety games in 1911.

But the man they were calling General Jackson played on, picking up the slack left by Lajoie's absence. In a morning game on the Fourth of July, Jackson came to bat in the sixth inning with one runner on base. The pitcher was Red Nelson of St. Louis. A shot to the outfield, a flubbed shoestring catch, and Jackson recorded his first and only inside-the-park home run.

All over American League ballparks the cries of "Give 'em Black Betsy, Joe. Give 'em Black Betsy!" were heard. And Joe Jackson gave them Black Betsy—in one extended midseason stretch of games he pounded away at a .462 clip.

Such achievement coexisted with ineptitude on major league playing fields that season. Bill Bergen concluded an eleven-year playing career spent with Brooklyn and Cincinnati with a .170 career batting average in 947 games—the lowest ever. With three weeks to go in the 1911 season, the Philadelphia Athletics won eleven of eighteen doubleheaders on their way to a World Series confrontation against the New York Giants, who won the first of three consecutive pennants in 1911.

For a time the great Cy Young was Jackson's teammate that season, but on August 15 he was released and signed by Boston. Young, who had hurled the first perfect game of the twentieth century in 1904 and had 511 career wins, the all-time record, pitched the final game of his career on September 7, 1911. The forty-four-year-old Young lost 1–0 to a rookie named Grover Cleveland Alexander. Young, Alexander, Walter Johnson, Christy Mathewson, Eddie Plank, Kid Nichols—each won more than 300 games in his career.

With just a few weeks left in the 1911 season, Jackson was batting .420, but his Cleveland team had no chance to win the pennant. Somers, who had become one of Jackson's favorite people in baseball, called him in for a talk.

JOE JACKSON: "Mr. Somers called me in to pay off, told me

I could sit it out for the rest of the season. I told him to wait until the season was ended and I wasn't quitting. I wrote my own contract the rest of the time I was in Cleveland."

At season's end Joe Jackson wound up batting .408, with 233 hits, 45 doubles, and 19 triples. Cleveland as a team hit 20 home runs, and Jackson had seven of them. He also had the career rookie year of the century, the only time a rookie ever batted .400.

Yet Jackson's lofty average didn't win him the batting title. Cobb won it using a unique split-hand batting grip that enabled him to move his top hand down if he wanted to pull the ball or push his bottom hand up when he wanted to go to left field. Cobb batted .420 in 1911.

All Jackson could claim was the highest runner-up season batting average of the twentieth century. Cobb, not satisfied with winning the batting title, went out of his way to mythologize the circumstances surrounding the batting race in various articles and in his autobiography. He even tried to change history, claiming that he had trailed Jackson for the batting-title lead. Then, he claimed, with all the resources and cunning at his disposal, cold-shouldering Jackson, taunting him, he was able to pull ahead in the final six games of the season.

JOE JACKSON: "A story that was heard a lot was that Ty Cobb bulldozed me by getting my goat in a conceived plan to ignore me in Cleveland in that important final series. That's just a lot of hooey. Ty was able to beat me out because he got more hits than I did."

The real facts are that after the first month Ty Cobb's batting average in 1911 was never below .400. After 80 games he was batting .450—70 points higher than Jackson. And 130 games into the season Jackson was at .398—18 points behind Cobb.

On October 2, with six games to go in the season, the Tigers and Cleveland met in a three-game series. Both men recorded three hits in the series, but Jackson got his in eight at bats while Cobb had ten official at bats. That tightened up the batting race even more, but Jackson was still about 14 points behind Cobb. In a kind of instant replay of his actions of the previous season against Nap Lajoie, Cobb decided to sit things out. He did not travel with the Tigers to St. Louis for the final three games of the season. His excuse was that for him to pad his batting average against the weak pitching of the lowly Browns was beneath his dignity.

Cleveland took the train to Chicago to finish out the season. Batting against Big Ed Walsh, Joe Jackson stroked three hits and was instrumental in Cleveland's victory, enabling the Naps to clinch third place. He did not play in the final game of the year—a game that had no significance for him or his team. Cleveland had third place; Cobb had another batting title.

TY COBB: "I had to fight all my life to survive. They were all against me . . . but I beat the bastards and left them in the ditch. . . . I was like a steel spring with a growing and dangerous flaw in it. If it is wound too tight or has the slightest weak point, the spring will fly apart and then it is done for."

Except for 1916, when Tris Speaker batted .386, Cobb won the American League batting championship each season from 1907 to 1919.

When Joe Jackson went back home to winter in South Carolina after his rookie season of 1911, he took his beloved bats along. "Bats don't like to freeze no more than me," he said, reflecting the obsessive intimacy with bats that had characterized baseball from the start. Players spent spare hours shaving, honing, heating, fondling, even sleeping with bats. Ty Cobb not only picked the wood for his bats, he also participated in their creation, honing away with a steer bone. Cap Anson allegedly hung bats like hams from the ceiling in the cellar of his house, and there were times the old baseballer had at least 500 pieces of lumber seasoning away. Always on the roam for good wood, Anson would sift through aged logs, shafts from carts, fence-posts, anything he could form into appropriate material for a baseball bat.

One of the more morbid stories about a baseball bat concerned a player named Perring. When the Ohio State Penitentiary was dismantled in 1880, he collected the hickory wood that had formed the prison's scaffolding. Perring fashioned the highly seasoned and strong timber into a bat that lasted nearly two decades.

Joe Jackson had about fifteen or twenty bats, and each one of them had a name. One he called Ol' Ginril, another was Caroliny. But his favorite was Black Betsy, that 48-ounce piece of lumber that he swung as easily as the 32-ounce bats used by some other players.

Jackson claimed that once when he was in a hitting slump, he pushed the end of his bat into some tar. As if by magic, he soon snapped out of his slump. From then on, all the top halves of his bats were black.

It was said that at the beginning of his career a moody and taciturn Jackson communicated more with his bats than he did with people. He would loll about in the dugout with the bat he would use that day, talking to it, telling it what he expected from it, what it had to do.

Sometimes other players were curious about Jackson and his bats. Once a teammate asked:

"Joe, what bats are you working with?"

"Big Jim, mostly."

"That bat's a new one on me."

"He's just a young fella, Big Jim, jes' a busher."

"I guess you're training him."

"Yeah, you're right. He's back in my room talkin' with Black Betsy right now."

The year of 1912 was one of endings and beginnings. The Tinker-Evers-Chance double-play combination played its final game together on April 12. The 1912 season saw brand-new baseball stadiums open—Fenway Park in Boston and Navin Field in Detroit. Both teams had a successful opening day on April 20. The Red Sox defeated the New York Yankees 7–6 in eleven innings, while the Tigers defeated Cleveland 6–5. That season Rube Marquard won a record nineteen straight for the New York Giants and went from "the $11,000 Lemon" to an $11,000 beauty.

On August 11, Joe Jackson became the second American League player to steal home twice in one game. In the first inning he stole home; in the seventh inning he stole second base, third base, and home. But it was the work he did with his bat that had everyone talking.

JACK ONSLOW: "I was a catcher with the Tigers that season of 1912 when Ty and Joe were running neck and neck for the batting championship. Cobb used to bench himself after he made a hit on his first time at bat to preserve his margin over Jackson. One day he told us how to pitch to Jackson and what do you think happened? Joe got three for three and drew closer to the batting lead."

He drew closer but never caught Cobb. Jackson batted .395 and rapped out 26 triples, an American League season record later tied by Sam Crawford. But Cobb hit .410 and again won the batting title. And Jackson gained the distinction of being the only player to bat over .390 for two years in a row yet not win a batting title.

JOE JACKSON: "What a hell of a league this is. I hit .387, .408, and .395 the last three years and I ain't won nothin' yet."

What he did win was the affection of the fans and most of the players on the Naps. As Jackson succeeded more and more on the playing field, his natural reticence began to erode and his sense of humor came to the fore. Those players on Cleveland who were playful or oddballs were enrolled in what was called the "Bug Club." Eddie Plank, Tris Speaker, and "Germany" Schaefer were prominent members. Easygoing Joe Jackson didn't know if it was a compliment or a putdown when he was appointed president.

BOB TARLETON, former baseball general manager: "A year or so after he joined Cleveland he was discouraged—he said they wanted to change his stance. That gave me a chuckle. In the opinion of all of his day, Joe was the most graceful batter in baseball. He stood motionless with both feet together until he was ready to swing. Then he took a stride. Most of the time the ball would be hit as straight as a clothes line."

JOE JACKSON: "I used to draw a line three inches out from the plate, from the front to the back of the plate every time I went to bat. I drew a right-angle line at the end next to the catcher and put my left foot on it exactly three inches from the plate. I kept both feet together and then took a long stride into the ball.

"When I was up there at the plate, my purpose was to get on base any way I could, whether by hitting or by getting hit or by a base on balls. If the hit-and-run was on I'd throw my bat at the ball if necessary to make a connection to keep from messing up a baserunner. I usually made the pitchers bear down and usually they all looked alike to me. I had no special spots where I could hit some pitchers better than others. I was in there swinging and if a pitch looked good enough to hit, I went for the ball, low, high, inside, or out if I had the sign from the manager to hit."

Jack Graney, a teammate of Jackson's in Cleveland who went on to become a popular broadcaster for the team, recalled:

"Jackson never seemed to know whether the pitcher was left-handed or right, or whether he hit a fastball, a curve, a spitter, or any of the trick deliveries. All he'd say, if you asked him, was that the ball was over. 'Over' for Jackson meant anything he could reach."

At bat Jackson was all focus, all business. Rarely did he ever complain about a call from an umpire. There were times, however, when he believed an umpire was mistaken. Then Jackson would simply turn and stare and then go about his business.

On March 4, 1913, the New York Yankees went to Bermuda, becoming the first team to go outside of the United States for spring training. Four days later the Federal League was organized. A six-team structure, the "outlaw loop" was poised to have a tremendous impact on major league baseball in the years ahead.

Baseball boomed that 1913 season; over 300 cities had professional teams. Minor league baseball attendance escalated. There were now forty leagues as opposed to thirteen in 1903.

In 1913, suffragettes attracted headlines marching on Washington. There were over 100,000 "lady typewriters"—

women employed in business offices. Everybody talked about the Gibson Girl: the vision of artist Charles Dana Gibson whose pen-and-ink magazine illustrations symbolized the ideal American girl in fashion and beauty. And at ballparks everywhere, although baseball was still a male-dominated preserve, women were coming out and attending games in larger numbers than ever before.

All over the United States "electrified" scoreboards were mounted outside of newspaper offices, bringing the baseball news to a fact-hungry public. In Times Square in New York City as many as 15,000 assembled at a time to watch the game "play out" on an 18-by-24 board that was suspended from the Times Building. The baseball was a celluloid ball; the players were represented by white lozenges.

Yet baseball in many ways still clung ceremoniously to its nineteenth-century roots. For instance, on June 30 of 1913, the Reds defeated the Cubs 9–6. One baseball was used for the entire game.

That season newspapers all over the country wrote about what Joe Jackson was able to do to a baseball. He led the American League in doubles, hits, and slugging percentage. He led his third-place Cleveland team with a .373 batting average. He finished ahead of all American League batters in hitting except for Ty Cobb. The Georgia Peach recorded a .390 average and another batting championship.

One of Jackson's great accomplishments in 1913 was a home run that he hit on June 4 over the right-field grandstand roof and out of the Polo Grounds. It was the first time anyone had ever done that. Years later, in retirement, Jackson would proudly show off the newspaper clips celebrating that moment—the longest home run ever measured at the Polo Grounds.

JACK GRANEY: "[Russell] Ford broke a low spitter at Jackson, and Joe literally golfed it clear over the top of the upper stand in right center field. It's 400 and something feet to the wall in that part of the Polo Grounds. And remember that the ball was a lump of coal in those days."

BOB TARLETON: "I managed a winter league club in New Orleans that offseason of 1913. We had three great outfielders: Joe Jackson, Detroit's Wahoo Sam Crawford, and Larry Gilbert, Brewer center fielder. We played once a week on Sundays. The clubs split the gate receipts—60 percent for winners and 40 percent for losers. The most Jackson ever collected was $7.20, the least $1.60. We played for fun in those days, not for money. Jackson was a soft-drink salesman on the side."

Working as salesmen on the side, lending their names and image to a product, good, or service—all was part of the scene in baseball right from the start. Tobacco tins like the one that featured Cy Young's likeness proclaimed the wonderful values of imbibing mild Havana tobacco. Tris Speaker and Joe Jackson modeled for ads for Boston Garters priced at 25 and 50 cents. The product was supposed to "hold your sock smooth as your skin." Joe Tinker posed self-consciously in an "Ide Silver" collar ad praising the merits of the product that sold two for 25 cents.

Throughout the era of ragtime, popular songs captured the attention of millions, who played them on pianos or sang them spontaneously at gatherings: "When You Wore a Tulip," "Down Among the Sheltering Palms," "Darktown Strutter's Ball," "I Never Knew I Could Love Anybody," "My Man," "Peg o' My Heart." One of Joe Jackson's favorite songs during his time with Cleveland was "I'm Sorry I Made You Cry." He would come up to the plate smiling, singing the title of the song. He only knew the words of the title; the rest of the song he hummed. Then he would wave his Black Betsy at the pitcher and laugh.

For a while, Jackson teamed up with Napoleon Lajoie, while Ty Cobb and Sam Crawford were a talented tandem for Detroit. Each of the players was something special in his own right. But as one-two batting punches, they rank among the best of all time.

JOE JACKSON: "Lajoie was the greatest hit-and-run batter in history. Batting in front of Nap for five years, I was able to see a master at work hitting behind the runner. And that ball was always hit so hard, it sounded like a bullet whizzing by me."

The Tigers, originally known as the Wolverines because Michigan is the Wolverine State, got their nickname because the black-and-brown stockings they wore reminded Manager George Stallings of tiger stripes. The team also was once known as the Detroit Creams because at one time they had the "cream of California baseball players." Neither Cobb nor Sam Crawford, another Tiger star, hailed from California, but they were the cream of American League baseball players.

Sam Crawford began his major league career with Cincinnati in 1899 and was nicknamed "Wahoo Sam" after his birthplace of Wahoo, Nebraska. While Jackson and Lajoie liked each other, Cobb and Crawford barely tolerated one another. As players, however, they were always in tune.

A familiar scene was Crawford coming to bat with Cobb on third base as the result of a triple or stolen bases. On many occasions Crawford would be walked, and on a signal from Cobb kick it into high gear, round first base, and streak for second while Cobb headed for home.

SAM CRAWFORD: "Sometimes they'd get him. Sometimes they'd get me. And sometimes they wouldn't get either of us."

One of the rare moments of frustration for Cobb and Crawford took place on June 25, 1914. St. Louis catcher Frank Crossin threw out Crawford attempting to steal second base, and the quick return throw to Crossin by Del Pratt nailed Cobb. A double play on an attempted double steal.

A specialty of the left-handed-hitting Crawford was gunning for home runs at League Park in Cleveland. The wire screen over the right-field wall had been placed there to hamper Crawford and others from hitting home runs out onto Lexington Avenue. He looked at the 45-foot barrier as a personal challenge. In the first series he played after the right-field wall had been remodeled at League Park, Crawford homered, placing the ball over the first exit gate.

But there was a Joe Jackson shot that old-timers talked about for years afterwards—a smash over the second exit gate, a distance of 326 feet. The ball left the field finally coming to rest on the other side of the street, a distance of another sixty feet. The 2,606 fans knew the ball was going to be a home run the instant Jackson swung, and if they didn't, a clear signal given by Tiger center fielder Hoffman dispelled any doubts. As the ball jumped off Black Betsy he threw up his hands in disgust.

Line drives against the left-field wall, shots belted to either side of the center fielder, blasts over the right-field wall that roared as they left the park—all were part of the Joe Jackson signature in Cleveland.

Who knows how many home runs Jackson might have recorded had the towering screen not been erected? It was hardly a move aimed against him; it was to please the fans in that era who delighted more in seeing a pitching duel than viewing balls hit out of the park.

While Lajoie and Crawford were mega-stars in their own right, it was the two southerners Jackson and Cobb who shared the American League spotlight. Ty Cobb was the "Georgia Peach" while Joe Jackson was the "Carolina Confection" and the "Candy Kid from Carolina." They were always compared.

"Jackson is Ty Cobb from the neck down," was a phrase always uttered by the Detroit star's supporters.

Manager Joe Birmingham of Cleveland said, "I would not trade Joe Jackson for Ty Cobb. I consider Joe the greater asset to the club of the two."

F.C. Lane, the editor of *Baseball Magazine,* wrote:

> Jackson is a better natural hitter by a considerable margin than Cobb who, as everyone knows, beats out many a leading hit. Jackson will be known in after-years as the man who might have been the greatest player the game has ever known. To sum up his talents is merely to describe in another way those qualities which should round out and complete the ideal player. In Jackson, nature has combined the greatest natural gifts any one player has ever possessed, but she denied him the heritage of early advantages and that well

balanced judgment so essential to the full development of his extraordinary powers.

Lane's comments were a none-too-thinly disguised reference to Joe Jackson's unpolished behavior and to the fact that he could neither read nor write.

On the road, Jackson would arrive at the hotel dining room for breakfast each morning, engage in an elaborate production of studying the menu with great care, and then in his pleasing Southern drawl say, "I guess I'll have the ham 'n' eggs." At dinnertime he would settle in at a table with a couple of his teammates, wait for them to order, and when hearing something that appealed to him say, "I guess I'll have the same."

Once served, Jackson would go after the food mainly with a knife. He had no need of a fork or spoon. Potatoes, pie, meat, salad—a knife and his fingers were all he used to get at the food. He never spoke when he ate; he would simply hunch over his plate and attack his meal.

For the long train trips, Jackson habitually purchased a lot of magazines. Once comfortably settled in, he would spend much time turning the pages, studying them carefully. Sometimes he would say out loud, "Boy, that was a good story," or, "What a swell idea that was."

A teammate would ask, "What was it all about?"

"Well, it's about a girl," Jackson would respond.

"What kind of girl?"

"Oh, you'll just to have to find out for yourself."

Soon after, he'd hurry off to the smoking car.

His illiteracy was an embarrassment to him and a malicious magnet for opposition fans. One day Jackson hammered out a triple. Standing on third base, he heard the catcalls and the familiar taunts asking him to spell simple words.

"Hey, Professor Jackson," one fan screamed, "can you spell 'cat'?"

Jackson spit out a huge plug of tobacco, stared the fan down, and shouted back, "Hey, big shot, can you spell shit?"

Others taunted him with "Shoeless Joe." He detested the nickname.

JOE WILLIAMS: "As a sportswriter, I knew Jackson, the ballplayer, well. I saw him play in the Southern League, and later as a Cleveland reporter, I traveled with him. He was pure country, a wide-eyed, gullible yokel. It would not have surprised me in those days to learn he had made a down payment on the Brooklyn Bridge."

Ben DeMott, one of the first college players in baseball, played briefly for Cleveland and had a locker right next to Jackson's. He disagreed with the assessment made by Williams.

BEN DeMOTT: "Aside from being a nearly perfect physical machine he had what few of the top-flight performers possessed. As long as I knew him he was never satisfied with his performance, although it seemed ridiculous to the kid who read his letters for him and who was also witness to the most remarkable displays of retentive memory anyone could imagine. Joe was far from stupid. He merely lacked education. I have often wondered if an education would not have taken much from his open-mindedness as well as cluttered up his uncanny memory. He could point to any rule in the book and 'read' it to you, but with enough ad-libbed words to indicate that he was reciting. He could do the same thing with an account of any game that his wife had read to him . . . I marvelled at that."

Wintering in South Carolina that offseason of 1913, Joe Jackson enjoyed the fruits of his growing popularity and business interests. Like other players, he began to engage in a growing and conspicuous consumerism. The automobile became their symbol of opulence; a fancy car was a clear indicator that they had made it. A spate of editorials expressed disapproval. *Baseball Magazine* said:

> It is, as a rule, a man's business how he spends his money. But nevertheless we wish to call attention to the fact that many men do so in an unwise manner. A very glaring instance of

this among baseball players is the recent evil tendency to purchase and maintain automobiles. Put the money away, boys, where it will be safe. You don't need those automobiles. The money will look mighty good later on in life. Think it over boys.

It was not just baseball players who were caught up in the tin-lizzy automobile craze. More and more, ordinary fans were driving cars. And many of them drove them to League Park. For some of those who owned homes close by the ballpark the cars provided a small source of revenue. Two and three cars could be parked on a lawn for 25 cents each.

The practice of color-coding tickets began at League Park in the 1914 season. Box seats were $1.25. Reserved seats were a dollar. General admission was seventy-five cents. For fifty cents fans gained admission to the pavilion, the double-decked grandstand extensions built between the original grandstand and the foul poles. A season ticket for an eight-seat box cost $100. Fans coming to the game on weekdays only had access to the park through the main gate on East 66th Street and Lexington Avenue. For those times when the park was especially crowded, another gate was made available. Ladies Days were designated to accommodate and encourage the growing interest in the sport by women. Anyone who purchased a grandstand ticket had the opportunity, at no charge, to bring along a lady.

The White Sox and Giants were two baseball teams that had a lot to talk about as the 1914 season got underway. Over the winter they had barnstormed on a world tour that included stops in Japan, Shanghai, Australia, France, and Egypt. They even had a command performance before the king of England.

On July 11, 1914, the Boston Red Sox faced Cleveland at Fenway Park. A moon-faced rookie named Babe Ruth made his first major league pitching start. The temperature in Boston was in the high seventies. Ruth was told not to worry too much about most of the Cleveland batters but to pay special attention to their cleanup hitter, Napoleon Lajoie, who crossed his back leg behind his front leg before he strode into a pitch. The Boston rookie was also told to be mindful of the third batter in the Cleveland lineup: Joe Jackson. Ruth handled Jackson pretty well in their first couple of head-to-head confrontations. Then, in the top of the seventh inning with Boston leading, Jackson came to bat again and ripped into one of the Babe's pitches to send it screaming out on a line. The game was tied 3–3. Ruth exited and was replaced by Dutch Leonard. Boston wound up winning the game 4–3.

The details of that game faded fast from Babe Ruth's memory, but the impression left on him by Joe Jackson lasted a very long time.

BABE RUTH: "I copied Jackson's style because I thought he was the greatest hitter I had ever seen, the greatest natural hitter I ever saw. He's the guy who made me a hitter. I copied his swing. I couldn't copy Ty Cobb's hand action because Ty was looking more for basehits than for power. Jackson stood with his feet fairly wide apart, his right foot shoved forward and the left foot back of the right. This gave him a good turn to start with. I changed this a little. I kept my feet closer together. I could get more leverage that way. But I was more easily caught off-balance by a left-hander. I had more trouble with left-handers than Joe ever had. He never had much trouble with anybody who threw a ball."

The big news in baseball that 1914 season was the play of the "Miracle Braves." In last place on July 19, they came on incredibly to win the National League pennant. But for Cleveland it was the same old story—another losing season. The team lost 102 games and finished dead last, 48½ games behind the pennant-wining Athletics, who won their fourth pennant in five years.

A special moment for Cleveland fans took place on September 27, when Napoleon Lajoie notched his 3,000th career hit in a game against the Yankees. It was a milestone moment in a fabled career winding down. A few months later Lajoie would be gone, picked up on waivers by the Philadelphia Athletics. With Lajoie gone, a local newspaper staged a contest to select a new nickname for the Cleveland team. The winning suggestion was Indians, to honor Cleveland Spider player Louis Francis Sockalexis, who had died in 1913. "The Chief," a Penobscot from Old Town, Maine, performed for Cleveland from 1897 to 1899 and was one of the first Native Americans to play in the majors.

Joe Jackson finished the 1914 season as the only .300 hitter on a team whose collective batting average was .245. His .338 batting average placed him fourth in the league behind Cobb, Eddie Collins, and Tris Speaker. All kinds of aches and pains and injuries that took a little longer to heal nagged at him throughout the season of 1914. And although he was still on the sweet side of thirty, he began to think more and more of life after baseball.

Offseasons once reserved for rest and reverie were now times for moneymaking, to top off the $6,000 or thereabouts of his Cleveland salary. Some of Jackson's funds were invested in business: a poolroom, a farm, a few dollars here and there to back other people's enterprises. He even went on the vaudeville circuit and performed a monologue: "A sob rendition," in the words of a writer of the time, "of his rise in the baseball world . . . from a minor piece in the cotton mill to a major place in the baseball world."

A *Sporting News* item of February 11, 1915, elaborated:

> It used to be the fashion to poke fun at Joe Jackson because he lacks an education, but whether Joseph knows his three Rs or not, he is getting by in this world and after a manner that puts some of his high brow critics to shame. Just now Joe is elevating the stage at a weekly salary that would make many a college professor sigh. He is doing a monologue telling how he plays ball and how he swings on the ball. He made his debut in Atlanta and has been booked for a tour of Southern cities provided he doesn't grow weary of the footlights. One thing Joe tells them is how he turned down $60,000 to play with the Feds for three years.

As the story goes, two agents for the Federal League came to Jackson's Greenville home and offered him a $25,000 cash deal—more than four times his Cleveland salary—to play for their Chicago franchise. They tempted him with promises of luxurious living. Resisting and recoiling at the blandishments, Jackson grabbed his Black Betsy bat and chased the agents away.

JOE JACKSON: "I felt I was duty-bound under contract to stick with Cleveland, and I can truthfully say, in all my playing days there and everywhere, I never shirked a duty to baseball."

Although he was getting worn down by losing, Jackson was comfortable in Cleveland. He and Katie spent many a summer night taking long walks through their residential neighborhood, often being invited in by neighbors for ice tea and rhubarb pie. They felt an affection for the city as well as an affinity for Charles Somers. Jackson especially liked the humane considerations the Cleveland owner exhibited to his players. Whenever the team played against the Senators in a weekend series in Washington where there was no Sunday ball, the Indians would board a train to Cleveland for a Sunday game and go back to Washington on Sunday night.

JOE JACKSON: "There wasn't a time we made that jump that Charlie Somers didn't come down the aisle of the train and give all the players twenty-dollar gold pieces."

Players who made the move to the Federal League received much more than gold pieces. But Jackson's turndown of the Feds further accentuated his farm-boy image. One wit quipped, "The Feds' mistake was in not showing Joe the money in pennies."

The Federal League had more than pennies when it began. Backed by millionaires, it started in 1912 as a minor league (the United States League) but collapsed after five weeks. The following year, with six teams managed by former major league stars, including Cy Young at Cleveland, the league finished a complete schedule of 120 games with teams in Chicago, Cleveland, Covington (Kentucky), Indianapolis, Pittsburgh, and St. Louis. Forty-one games into the season, the Covington franchise switched to Kansas City. In 1914, the Federal League declared itself a major league, added two new teams, and the war was officially on.

Big money men supplied the cash for the Federal League: Robert B. Ward of Brooklyn's Ward banking empire and Tip-Top Bread fortune; Oklahoma oilman Harry Sinclair, later convicted in the Teapot Dome scandal; Charles A Gilmore, wealthy Chicago coal merchant who became president of the Federal League; Philip D.C. Ball, manufacturer of ice machinery in St. Louis; and Otto Stifel, a St. Louis brewer. They along with other wealthy owners enabled their teams to sign up more than eighty major leaguers.

One of the first to jump to the Federal League was Joe Tinker. A shortstop for the Reds in 1913, Tinker wanted a piece of his price of $15,000 when he was sold to Brooklyn. When his demand was denied he jumped, doubling his salary by becoming player-manager of the Chicago Whales. Other stars recruited by the rival league included Eddie Plank, "Three Finger" Brown, Claude Hendrix, Chief Bender, Howie Camnitz, Otto Knabe, Ed Reulbach, Hal Chase, George Mullin, and Jim Delahanty.

The Chicago Whales, who featured outfielder Dutch Zwilling, were one of the more successful teams; they finished in second place in 1914, in first place in 1915, and challenged the major league's pennant winners, only to be rebuffed. Benny Kauff, called "the Ty Cobb of the Federal League," won the batting title both years of the league's existence and was a two-time stolen-base leader. "He has enough money to start a bank," was how his local newspaper in Middletown, Ohio, put it—an allusion to the high salary paid to one of the Federal League's top draws.

The great Walter Johnson was almost a Federal Leaguer, too. Offered a $16,000 salary by the Chicago Whales—$4,000 more than his Washington team was prepared to pay, plus a $10,000 signing bonus—Johnson was set to jump. Senators owner Clark Griffith went to Chicago and spoke with White Sox owner Charles Comiskey. "If Johnson signs with the

Whales," he said, "how would you like to see him pitching on the north side and drawing away all your fans from the south side of Chicago?" Comiskey peeled off $10,000; Walter Johnson remained a Senator. The Federal League offered to double the salaries of Ty Cobb and Sam Crawford if they switched allegiance, but the two Tiger stars declined the lucrative offers.

While the new circuit had some high moments, any real success for the Federal League was doomed from the start. Establishment newspapers condemned it. *The Sporting News* claimed that its players placed "money before honor."

In January of 1915 an antitrust suit filed by what many were calling "the outlaw league" against the major leagues was placed before Judge Kenesaw Mountain Landis's Northern Illinois Federal District Court. In many historical ways the suit set a kind of precedent for the one to be filed seventy years later by the United States Football League against the National Football League.

Since Landis was known as a hardliner against monopolies, Federal League officials and owners thought they would have a responsive ear for their complaint that major league baseball formed a monopoly that controlled the business of interstate baseball.

But strangely, Landis kept procrastinating and delaying his decision. He made a point of declaring how unwilling he was to damage America's national pastime.

JUDGE LANDIS: "Both sides must understand that any blows at the thing called baseball would be regarded by this court as a blow to a national institution."

The Landis delay triggered rising Federal League court costs. The legal footdragging plus dropping attendance sapped the Federal League's treasury. By the end of the first season losses were put at $176,000; the Indianapolis Hoosiers, winners of the 1914 pennant, collapsed.

For 1915, amid much regrouping, there was optimism that the Federal League would make a go of it. The second season began with much fanfare: parades, free tickets, all types of high-powered promotions, more marquee players added to rosters (Chief Bender, who had posted a 17–3 record with the 1914 Philadelphia Athletics, went 4–16 for Baltimore). But the Federal League dream was not to be. Despite teams like Brooklyn opening their gates providing free admission, Federal League baseball couldn't be given away. By the end of the 1915 season, Robert Ward, the league's most powerful supporter, died. The rest of the owners were ready to bail out.

In an out-of-court "peace settlement" on December 22, the major leagues permitted the owners of the Chicago Whales, Charles Weeghman and Harry Sinclair, to purchase controlling interests in the Chicago Cubs. Sinclair was also "paid off" at the rate of $10,000 a year for a decade by the major leagues as balm for the demise of his Federal League holdings. St. Louis businessman Phil Ball was allowed to purchase the St. Louis Browns. Money passed hands as Federal League owners were paid for their players and given hundreds of thousands of dollars for their interests in their franchises. The total settlement paid to the Federal League by the majors was about $5 million. It was truly hush money, enabling major league baseball to skirt the issues of the reserve clause, being a monopoly, and restraint of trade.

Much of the skirting came as a result of Landis's stalling tactics, which went a long way towards enhancing his image with major league owners and put him in their debt. *The Sporting News* ran a two-column photo of the judge captioned, "He's the game's good friend." That was all that had to be said.

Most players went back to their original major league teams. The Giants were able to acquire Benny Kauff, and the Cubs picked up the top Federal League slugger, Dutch Zwilling.

By 1916, the Federal League was a footnote to baseball history, and so were its teams: the Chicago Whales, St. Louis Terriers, Pittsburgh Rebels, Kansas City Packers, Newark Peppers, Buffalo Blues, Brooklyn Tip-Tops, and the Baltimore Terrapins. The league would tarry in memory through a liquor named for it, Federal League Bourbon Whiskey, and a ballpark built for its Chicago franchise: Wrigley Field. And for baseball card collectors, it still survives in two sets of cards issued in 1914 and

1915. These cards were not produced by tobacco companies as was the vogue. Instead they were distributed by Cracker Jacks, an additional wrinkle adding to their uniqueness.

Preseason 1915 gossip about Joe Jackson and his off-the-field activities revealed a different side to his personality. He was so caught up in touring around the south with "Joe Jackson's Baseball Girls," a musical vaudeville farce, that newspapers reported that he was unable and unwilling to report to spring training with Cleveland. It was rumored he was also caught up in an affair with one of his "Girls."

A newspaper reported on April 15, 1915:

> Joe Jackson's admirers have been much put out by that worthy's recent actions. It seems that Joe so misbehaved that his wife threatened to sue for divorce. She sent a deputy sheriff after Joseph, had him brought home and gave him another chance. He has agreed to take it, and the hope is that he will permanently regain his senses. It's the old case of too much prosperity. From a shoeless butcher's boy who didn't know his ABCs to a popular star feted by fans and fawned upon by chorus girls, was too much for Joe's mental makeup and he temporarily lost his balance.

Jackson finally regained his balance and reported very late to spring training with Cleveland. He was soon back in his familiar routine. That spring of 1915 headlines in major league baseball included the Athletics' Herb Pennock coming within one out of an Opening Day no-hitter, the five errors committed by the newly signed Philadelphia baseman, Nap Lajoie, and the first major league home run hit on May 6, 1915, by Red Sox pitcher Babe Ruth in the third inning in a game at the Polo Grounds off New York's Jack Warhop.

As July moved into August, Jackson kept on slashing the ball and making big plays in the outfield for Cleveland, a team whose downward spiral showed no signs of ending. In 1911, the team had finished in third place, 22 games off the pace. The following year it dropped to fifth, 30½ games out. In 1913, it ended up in third place, 9½ games out, and in 1914, it was dead last, a staggering 48½ games out of first. Now in 1915, not only did the Indians have trouble winning games, they faced the problem of drawing fans and paying bills. As one of the weakest teams in the majors, Cleveland was hit especially hard by the challenge of the Federal League.

On August 21, 1915, Charley Somers, desperate to make a move and do something to reverse his negative cash flow, traded Joe Jackson to the Chicago White Sox. In return Cleveland received outfielders Robert "Braggo" Roth and Larry Chappell, pitcher Ed Klepfer, and $31,500. It was one of the highest cash transactions to that time for a major leaguer.

Through years of changing fortune with Cleveland, and through the tenure of five different managers—Deacon McGuire, George Stovall, Harry Davis, Joe Birmingham, and Lee Fohl—Joe Jackson had been the one constant. In 673 games he had batted .374; 400 of his 937 hits were for extra bases. Now he was gone.

Cleveland fans were angry and disappointed. First the legendary Napoleon Lajoie had departed. Now the most popular player on their team, a superstar who was hitting .331, was gone as well.

While gloom pervaded Cleveland, in Chicago there was glee. Charles A. Comiskey bragged that his White Sox "now had the greatest straightaway hitter in all of baseball."

[4]

Chicago

In the 1880s Charles Albert Comiskey, the man they called the Old Roman, was a first baseman-manager who led the St. Louis Browns to four straight pennants in the American Association. When the century turned, Comiskey, a self-made millionaire, returned to his native Chicago and became owner-president of the windy city's American League entry. The Chicago White Stockings, the original name of the franchise, was shortened to White Sox by sportswriters Carl Green and I.E. Sanborn to fit headlines.

In 1901, the White Sox won the American League pennant under Clark Griffith. In 1906, the Sox came up against their crosstown rivals the Chicago Cubs in what was known as the "horseless carriage" World Series. The Cubs under player-manager Frank Chance had won 116 regular-season games, the highest total in baseball history, but they went down to defeat at the hands of the White Sox. In the following seven years, however, the Sox did not win. Defeat prodded Comiskey to make many moves on and off the field in his quest for a championship, hiring and firing five managers in the first eleven years of his team's existence.

On July 1, 1910, the American League Chicago team began play in brand-new White Sox Park, a facility that would last until 1990. The *Reach Baseball Guide* recalled the time: ". . . a gala day in the city of Chicago, and a red-letter day in the eventful life of the white-haired chief of the American League club.

The afternoon witnessed the formal opening and dedication of the White Sox's new ball park, and the evening was devoted to official celebration of the historical event by a great banquet at which a host of notables, including most of the grandees of the baseball world were the guests of Comiskey."

A recordbreaking crowd marveled at the thousands of yards of brilliant bunting that adorned the park for the opening game between the White Sox and the St. Louis Browns. A newspaper of the time called the new stadium ". . . without hesitation and without invidious comparison . . . the finest ball park in the United States."

Located on the south side of Chicago at 35th and Shields and nicknamed the "Baseball Palace of the World," it was a splendid edifice. The steeples of several churches, the facades of brand-new buildings, and the languid leafiness of old trees formed a pleasing backdrop. A symmetrical park with a single-deck grandstand extending from right field to left field, the stadium would be renamed Comiskey Park in 1913 in honor of its powerful owner. The foul lines stretched out 362 feet and the center-field wall was 420 feet away from home plate. The park had been built on the site of a former city dump. Its foul lines were old water hoses that were painted white and flattened out. A green cornerstone was laid on St. Patrick's Day in 1910; it would stay that color until 1960 when Bill Veeck had the entire exterior of the park painted white. Directly east of the stadium stood a small wooden grandstand once used by the Chicago Pirates, the city's entry in the short-lived Players' League, the major league created in 1890 by the Brotherhood of Professional Ball Players. Charles Comiskey had played first base for the Pirates.

Many unusual features were included in the new stadium, which some likened to the ancient Roman Coliseum. Comiskey said the fans were really the ones who built the park, so he had showers installed in the bleachers behind center field to aid them in their efforts to cope with the sweltering Chicago summer. There were picnic areas, including "Bullring" in left and "Bullpen I and II" in right and right-center field. There were

Bavarian and Mexican restaurants and beer halls under the stands behind the plate.

Comiskey showed consideration for the fans by allowing any legitimate Chicago group to use his ballpark for outings, meetings, festivals—free of charge. He extended a lavish hand to the working press, fawning over reporters, cultivating them, providing them with plenty of food and drink at Comiskey Park, and inviting them to his private club in Wisconsin, dubbed Woodland Bards.

On November 13, 1913, the White Sox and Giants began a celebrated world baseball tour that was highlighted by a special exhibition game played before England's King George in London. The teams played fifty-six games in Japan and Egypt, Rome, Sri Lanka, and many other exotic venues. Flushed and buoyed by the receptions he received, Comiskey started making moves to build a White Sox baseball dynasty.

After nearly a month of rumors, on December 8, 1914, the White Sox owner spent $50,000 and obtained second baseman Eddie Collins from the Philadelphia Athletics. Collins was regarded by most experts as the greatest position player of that era. The deal broke up Connie Mack's $100,000 infield. Called "Cocky" because of his confidence, Collins's Ivy League education was a rarity among the players of his time.

With Collins in the fold and signed to a guaranteed five-year contract, Comiskey went about bragging that he was putting together the "best team ever." There would be five new position players on the 1915 team, including promising minor leaguer Happy Felsch, purchased from Milwaukee in the minors. The five would be added to a trio of talented young players—pitcher Red Faber, catcher Ray Schalk, and infielder Buck Weaver.

Nine days after acquiring Collins, Comiskey made more headlines. He reached down to Peoria and hired thirty-three-year-old minor league executive and coach Clarence "Pants" Rowland as White Sox manager. Rowland was young, but so were the Sox.

On August 21, 1915, Joe Jackson became another piece of

the changing team ethos that was the Chicago White Sox, his third major league team in six years. Just about a week before, the White Sox had purchased the contract of minor league pitcher Claude "Lefty" Williams.

The Joe Jackson who joined Chicago was a very different person from the one who had reluctantly reported to the Cleveland American League club more than half a decade before. Although he liked Cleveland as a city and had made many friends there, he had been frustrated by the losing times. He knew the White Sox were loaded with talent and looked forward to the chance to play in a World Series and to garner the fame and financial rewards accompanying that opportunity.

The accents of the South were still with him, and he still looked for rusty pins and stuck them into the back pocket of his uniform pants. He still lavished loving treatment on Black Betsy. He even used his bat to help increase suppleness and strength in his arms and wrists. For more than an hour at a time, Jackson would hold the bat by the handle, his arm outstretched as far as possible. Then he would switch the bat to his other hand and do it all over again. He also kept to his ritual of eye exercises that consisted of his staring with one eye at a lit candle in a dark room until he could barely make out the vision. Then he would go through the same procedure with his other eye. The powerfully built Jackson claimed the procedure not only exercised his eyes but also helped him to pick up a pitched or batted ball better.

In most ways he had stayed the same throughout the years; it was only in his outward appearance that most noticed a change. His teeth had been straightened and cleaned up. For special occasions he now wore thirty-dollar pink silk shirts, and four-dollar Arrow shirts for normal wear. He had a collection of shoes of all types, many of them shiny patent-leather ones. The shoe fetish might have been triggered by self-consciousness over the "Shoeless Joe" label that still clung to him, a label he loathed but could not shed.

That whole time during the 1915 season when the White Sox were at home Jackson did not suit up with the other Chicago players. Instead he came to the park in uniform straight from the hotel where Comiskey had arranged for him to stay.

Jackson found Chicago a lot different from Cleveland. It was a city on the edge, a polygot, ugly, muscular mass of people, places, and plans. Its brick pavements where horse-drawn wagons and cars vied for space symbolized an old century dying and a new one beginning its crest. In Chicago, it all came together: racial tensions, union tensions, the shimmy and the shake, sex and crime and women on the prowl, men and boys looking for trouble, and trouble looking for them. The South Side, where the ballpark of the Chicago American League team was located, was a sprawl of smells, sounds, and sights—a market of goods and services of every kind.

Jackson was pleased to be reunited with Eddie Collins, with whom he had played in Philadelphia. The move elated Collins, always a big booster of Jackson.

EDDIE COLLINS: "I've seen the best players the past twenty years, and no one has been better than Joe Jackson, who instinctively does everything right on the playing field. I can't recall Jackson missing a signal from the bench or coach, when he was at bat or on the bases. And he always threw the ball in from the outfield to the right spot. And how he could throw."

While Collins appreciated Jackson's skills as a player, Jackson was virtually in awe of Collins as player and personality. Always referring to the brilliant second baseman as "Mr. Collins," Jackson was the most attentive listener to the motivational lectures Collins gave on "Inside Baseball."

JOE JACKSON: "Eddie Collins was the smartest man that ever walked on a ball field. He did our thinking for us. He figured out what was going to happen before it happened. Once he told me to play out over on the left-field foul line for Babe Ruth. I asked him why. I could move ten feet, you know, after a ball, and I couldn't figure why. Eddie said Babe was going to hit over third base that day, and he wanted me to be all set. I stood almost on the foul line. Babe hit a smash right into my hands that would have won the ballgame."

With the addition of Collins and Jackson, Comiskey felt he

had a team to bring back the glory days of the White Sox. Comiskey continued to call Jackson "the greatest straightaway hitter in baseball" and bragged to everyone that he was paying him $10,000 a year. Jackson was actually earning $6,000, but what was a $4,000 difference, anyway? The higher figure had a much grander ring.

Comiskey believed in spending money on the working press and on acquiring top talent. But his lavishness ended when it came to paying his players. Those on other teams received four dollars a day for meals; Comiskey, of whom it was said "he threw nickels around for players like they were manhole covers," doled out three dollars a day. He also charged players 50 cents for cleaning their uniforms. Those players who rebelled and played in soiled uniforms had them taken from their lockers and cleaned. For these laundry services Comiskey docked them additional change for each item.

In his first at bat for Chicago at Comiskey Park, in a game against the New York Yankees with a runner at first base, Jackson took a level swing with Black Betsy and rifled a shot against the right-field wall. His personal streak of getting a hit the first time up with every team he ever played for was intact. But despite some heroic moments like this first at bat for Chicago, Jackson hit just .265 for the White Sox in forty-six games and wound up with the lowest season batting average of his career—.308. Difficulty adjusting to new surroundings was part of his personality profile. The schisms and cliques on Chicago also made him feel disoriented.

His high hopes of being in a World Series had not yet been realized, but his new team won 93 games in 1915 and posted a winning percentage of .604—229 points better than Cleveland, who finished in seventh place. The White Sox climbed to third in 1915, a season that saw Ty Cobb steal 96 bases, a record that stood until 1962, when Maury Willis stole 104.

As the 1916 season got under way Jackson was more determined than ever to have a big year. His .308 batting average of the year before was an embarrassment to him. So was an article in *Baseball Magazine* published in March of 1916 entitled

"The Man Who Might Have Been the Greatest Player in the Game."

In the first few games they played that 1916 season, the White Sox showcased the skills and versatility that made it clear that the team was a coming powerhouse. On the first day of the season Jackson gunned down a Red Sox runner at third base with a throw from deep left field. It was a dramatic demonstration of why they referred to his glove as "the place where triples go to die." The throw especially impressed catcher Ray Schalk, who had joined the White Sox in 1912 and was on his way to an eighteen-year Hall of Fame career.

On April 15, Schalk, the man they called "Cracker," impressed Jackson and the rest of the White Sox players. Schalk stole two bases on his way to a season total of thirty, setting a record that would stand for catchers until John Wathan stole thirty-six in 1982. Just 5′ 9″ and 165 pounds, Schalk was a workhorse behind the plate and one of the reasons the White Sox pitching staff was so successful.

The White Sox faced Cleveland on June 26. Jackson kidded some of his old teammates about the numerals on their uniform sleeves, the first time players ever were identified with numbers corresponding to the scorecard. Then he proceeded to play against some of his old friends with all the verve and vitality he could muster. Playing all out against every team was his way, but the fact that he had been sold by Cleveland gave him additional incentive.

In Chicago, Jackson was a magnet for kids, who flocked around him after a game. They waited for him to emerge from the grounds and fought for the privilege of carrying his bats. Jackson was like a kid himself. His youthful fans would greet him, and he would respond by calling many of them by their names. Sometimes he would stop by a vacant lot near the park, take out a practice ball from his pocket, and toss it to the kids, playing catch with them. Sometimes he would hit a ball far over the railroad tracks. For many days afterward the youth who retrieved the ball would show it off to his friends, a treasured keepsake.

Joe Jackson garnered perhaps the most attention by showing off the throwing power of his arm. Standing with his back to the left-field wall in Comiskey Park, he was able to throw a ball over the grandstand behind home plate. The fans had a name for what Jackson did—"showouts" they were called.

By the time the Fourth of July of 1916 rolled around Jackson was staging a fireworks celebration all his own. Hitting out of that famous pigeon-toed batting stance and going three for five against Philadelphia on Independence Day, he capped an incredible hitting string that saw him rap out 55 hits in 104 at bats in a thirty-game stretch that had begun on May 31. His batting average during that dazzling exhibition of hitting was .524.

Katie, as she had been in Cleveland, was a regular at all the Chicago games and sometimes traveled with the team. With the cliques on the club, it was comforting for Jackson to have her around. Newspapers referred to her as "The White Sox Girl" and the "White Sox Mascot."

On the road Jackson roomed with a fellow southerner, the rookie pitcher Lefty Williams. A part of his milieu and yet apart from it, Joseph Jefferson Jackson attempted to cover up his country ways with city-slicker garb—flashy clothes and always the most expensive shoes. His facade had changed but inside he was still the same. He carried a five-gallon jug of corn liquor with him at all times. And one of his favorite hotel-room activities was getting into bed and eating animal crackers that he washed down with the corn liquor.

JOE WILLIAMS: "In keeping with his growing eminence he demanded and got a drawing room for road trips. He was a drinker but not a heavy one. He carried his own tonic: triple distilled corn. And on occasions he carried a parrot, a multicolored pest who had mastered a few salty dugout phrases. One of these was 'You're out.' Another was 'You're lousy, O'Loughlin.' O'Loughlin was an umpire."

Jackson commented on the parrot: "The kid's got more brains than the old man."

New York, Philadelphia, Washington, Cleveland, Boston, Detroit, and St. Louis—Jackson traveled around the American

League circuit. The brass spitoons in the hotel foyers and lobbies, the beds welded from brass that he slept on—it was all becoming a ceremony to him.

The 1916 Sox were described by *Chicago Tribune* columnist "Si" Sanborn as neither "fish, fowl, nor good red herring." The team had a lot of talent but inconsistent play dogged it all season. Under .500 until the end of June, they reached first place on August 3, stayed there a week and then were overtaken by the Red Sox, powered by the pitching of Babe Ruth, league ERA leader and winner of twenty-three games.

Norman Rockwell did his first *Saturday Evening Post* cover in 1916. It was little noticed compared with all the exciting things happening in baseball. Fans were caught up in the New York Giants' record twenty-six game winning streak from September 7 to September 30 and the last hurrahs of Christy Mathewson and Mordecai "Three Finger" Brown. Both baseball immortals pitched the final game of their careers on September 4—against each other in the second game of a doubleheader in Chicago. Before the game the old adversaries were each presented with a bouquet of American Beauty roses. Mathewson's Cincinnati team outlasted Brown's Chicago club, 10–8.

The once-mighty Philadelphia Athletics lost twenty straight games in one stretch that 1916 season on their way to a last-place finish. The now-mighty White Sox finished in second place, just two games behind Boston. Jackson's hitting heroics were a major reason for his team's excellent season. He had a banner year—third in the league with a batting average of .341, first in total bases and triples, second in slugging percentage and hits, third in doubles, fifth in RBIs.

There was a hunger in Joe Jackson to succeed on the baseball field; there was also a powerful drive in him to acquire and indulge himself in the good things in life. The early years of doing without, the clothing patched and repatched and worn year after year, the grinding sounds of the mill that he sometimes heard in his sleep—all of these had shaped Joe Jackson. Contrary to the "stupid hick" label that he somehow could never shed, he had a lot of business acumen and common sense.

Joe Jackson had become so enmeshed in commercial enterprises that he was virtually a mini-conglomerate. He was the owner of part of a poolroom in Greenville, a farm, and the best house in West Greenville, which he had purchased as a gift for his parents. The poolroom and the farm would fail, but he told people that "you had to lose some to make some."

He owned the "Baseball Girls," which toured the Southern vaudeville loop. He also organized a barnstorming team featuring his five brothers and two first cousins. Money also came in from endorsements like the one that depicted him fashionably dressed behind the wheel of an automobile in a newspaper advertisement with the slogan: "The Oldsmobile Eight for me every time."

When the 1916 season ended, he purchased a house for $10,000 on the Savannah waterfront. From the time Jackson had played in Savannah, he had always harbored an affection for that lovely city. That, coupled with the fact that his sister Lula had married and moved there, clinched his decision to take up residence in Savannah.

There were those who wondered why Jackson did not reside in Chicago year-round and capitalize on his growing popularity there.

JOE JACKSON: "If all my business interests were not down South, I reckon I'd live up here in the north all the time."

His response was diplomatic but evasive. He was a man of the South, comfortable there, accepted there.

Five days before the opening of the 1917 season, the final season of future Hall of Famers Honus Wagner, Eddie Plank, Johnny Evers, and Sam Crawford, the United States declared war on Germany. Hank Gowdy, a catcher for the Boston Braves, was the first major leaguer to enlist in the United States Armed Forces.

War fever was everywhere. It made players like Heinie Zimmerman and Heinie Groh change their first names to Henry. Resolutions were passed by the National and American Leagues mandating an hour a day of military drill for players. Teams balked at the idea but went along; only iconoclastic Brooklyn refused to cooperate. Beginning in spring training and continuing throughout the season, the close-order drills consisted of players—their bats mounted on their shoulders instead of rifles—supervised by Army sergeants. Ban Johnson put up $500 as a prize in a competition for the best-drilled team, which turned out to be the hapless St. Louis Browns.

Spring training sites for most teams were closer to home to economize on railroad travel. As the season moved through its ritual of April, May, June, and summer into fall, games were interrupted for the selling of war bonds and baseball would be exported to Germany, England, Belgium, Italy, France, and even Guam. Each major league team sported on its uniform some type of badge or shield that reflected patriotism; red, white, and blue shields and American flags sewn onto uniform shirt fronts were most common.

A wet and cold spring impacted dramatically on the new season, causing the National League to postpone forty-eight games the first month of the season. American participation in World War I, however, had a more profound effect than the bad weather. The government ordered all horse racing suspended until the end of the war; baseball was allowed to continue. With racetracks closed down, gamblers seeking another outlet to ply their trade turned their attention to the national pastime. The lobbies of hotels where major league teams stayed became conspicuous congregating places for gamblers and their assorted retinue. And they vied with each other for the bragging rights to which games and which players they had been able to fix.

That 1917 season White Sox manager Pants Rowland and owner Charles A. Comiskey bragged about the prospects of their team. The catching position was solid with fiery Ray Schalk, who would catch a major league record four no-hitters in his career. Schalk's career batting average would be only .253, the lowest of any nonpitcher in the Hall of Fame. But he was a player who revolutionized the catcher's position, innovating the now routine procedure of backing up plays behind first and third to protect against a wild throw.

Swede Risberg and veteran first baseman Charles Arnold Gandil, better known as "Chick," were newcomers to the 1917 Chicago roster. Acquired from Cleveland for $3,500 on February 25, 1917, Gandil actually was a member of the White Sox in 1910, but only lasted part of the year and was sold to the Washington Senators. His circle of friends included Sport Sullivan, a bookie and gambler with mob connections. Gandil had run away from home at age seventeen to compete in baseball in the rough towns along the Mexican border. He picked up $150 a fight by boxing in the local heavyweight division to supplement his baseball wages. He was a big man, 6'2" and a well-built 200 pounds. Paid just $4,000 in 1917, Gandil and the truculent Swede Risberg, who earned $2,500 that year, were at the low end socioeconomically on the Sox.

The rough and rangy man they called "Swede" had a flashy style, a powerful arm, and a quick temper. In the minors he had once kayoed an umpire with just one punch after a dispute over a called third strike. The arrival of Risberg at shortstop for the White Sox in 1917 allowed Buck Weaver to move back to third base, his natural position.

Hawk-faced Buck Weaver was born George Daniel Weaver on August 19, 1890, in Pottstown, Pennsylvania. A switch-hitter, he was such a nimble fielder that it was said that even Ty Cobb would not bunt against him. Weaver's hallmarks were his smiling face and his mincing steps closer and closer to the batter—body language daring the bunt.

Second baseman Eddie Collins may have been the best ever at his position. In 1917, he was at the midpoint and prime of his twenty-five-year career in the majors. A left-handed batter, Collins could bunt, slash away at the ball, or hit and run. It was his intelligence and poise, however, that set him above virtually all the players of his time and enabled him to make plays in the field that many thought were impossible.

Center fielder Happy Felsch possessed almost as much range as the great Tris Speaker. A native of Milwaukee, Felsch had a passion for baseball, silly riddles, off-color jokes, and any kind of whiskey. Felsch attracted attention for his range in the outfield and powerful throwing arm. His given names were Oscar Emil, but "Happy" characterized his personality—always smiling and ready for a good time. It was this nature that compelled him to throw in with the more earthy members of the White Sox.

Right field was capably manned by right-handed batting Shano Collins, who was in his seventh season with the White Sox in 1917. A defensive specialist and fine all-around athlete, he hit against left-handed pitching while Nemo Leibold, a southpaw swinger, batted against right-handers. Leibold's given names were Harry Loran. But his small size—5' 7" and 157 pounds—earned him the Nemo nickname that derived from the comic-strip character "Little Nemo."

On the mound, Chicago had three of the best in the game. Catcher Ray Schalk bragged about how much fun it was to catch pitchers Ed Cicotte, Red Faber, and Lefty Williams.

A native of Detroit, Eddie Cicotte began his major league career in 1905 with his home-town team. The following year he moved on to the Red Sox. On July 22, 1912, he was sold to the White Sox. Deception on the mound was his game, as was pinpoint control and the ability to change speeds. The St. Louis Browns saw Cicotte's whole bag of tricks on April 14, 1917, when he no-hit them 11–0.

Spitballer Red Faber was born in Cascade, Iowa, in 1886 and joined the White Sox in 1914. There he would remain for twenty years, winning 254 games and winding up as a member of the Baseball Hall of Fame in 1964.

Claud "Lefty" Williams was born in Aurora, Missouri, but lived in the South. In 1916, his first year with the White Sox, he had won 13 of 20 decisions. He was a moody and inarticulate type.

On the sixth of June this all-star cast moved into first place in the American League standings. They would trade places at the top with the Boston Red Sox through the rest of that month. On June 23, the Red Sox were involved in one of the most unusual games ever played. Ernie Shore of Boston relieved Babe Ruth, who was tossed out of the game after he walked the first batter and got into an argument with umpire Clarence "Brick" Owen. The baserunner was caught stealing, and Shore retired the next twenty-six batters, pitching a perfect game. Shore was one of the most successful pitchers of the era. Like many of his contemporaries, he marveled at Joe Jackson's skill with a bat.

ERNIE SHORE: "Everything he hit was really kissed. He could break bones with his shots. Blindfold me and I could still tell you when Joe Jackson hit the ball. It had a special crack."

JOE WOOD: "You tried your best and hoped it wasn't his day."

CHIEF BENDER: "Pitching to him made me feel like an ass."

ED WALSH: "Jackson hit the ball harder than any man that ever played in the big leagues and I don't mean except Babe Ruth."

Pitchers strained for adjectives to describe what it was like going head to head against Joe Jackson and his Black Betsy. Holding his hands down at the bottom of his bat, the little finger of his right hand curled around the knob, taking a full cut, Jackson rarely struck out. His flawless, whiplash left-handed swing was the envy of all the hitters of his time, including Babe Ruth and Ty Cobb.

TY COBB: "Joe's swing was purely natural, he was the perfect hitter. He batted against spitballs, shineballs, emeryballs and all the other trick deliveries. He never figured anything out or studied anything with the same scientific approach I gave it. He just swung. If he'd ever had any knowledge of batting, his average would have been phenomenal. Chances are Joe could've learned to bunt and beat out slow bounders to the infield because he was fast enough, the same as I did, but he seemed content to just punch the ball, and I can still see those line drives whistling to the far precincts. Joe Jackson hit the ball harder than any man ever to play baseball. What's more, he would have gone down as the greatest batter of all time had he made a study of the scientific side of the batting art."

Cobb's statement was not exactly on target; Jackson did adjust to some pitchers and circumstances when he was up there at the plate. Against the flamethrowing Walter Johnson, Jackson never took a full cut. He moved his bat forward in more of a half-swing, seeking to neutralize the Big Train's fast stuff. It worked. There were some estimates that in his career Jackson batted close to .500 against Johnson.

JOE JACKSON: "No doubt in my mind, Walter Johnson was the fastest pitcher of all time . . . but my career batting average against him was .475. How did I manage to connect against his fastball? Why, I just pecked at him. . . . The only way you could hit him was to poke the ball. I used to wait for his curves. Used to kid him by standing up straight with the bat leaning against my hip. Walter wouldn't hit a batter if he could possibly keep the ball away from him.

"I recall one game that I broke up against Johnson and Washington with a home run. As I jogged around the bases I said to Johnson in all sincerity: 'Tough luck, Walter, I guess it just had to happen.' And the big fellow replied: 'Ain't nothing tough about it. You just know how to hit.'

"Yep, I guess I used to hit Johnson pretty good. . . .But I had to smarten up on him. He's the only pitcher who ever made me choke up on my bat, and I never tried to poke him for anything more than a single."

WALTER JOHNSON: "Jackson didn't seem to have a weakness. I was always glad when he had been disposed of without having him break up the game. . . . He gave me more trouble than anyone else. I always figured I was in a hole whenever Jackson came up there. He was always looking down your throat ready to hit the ball. Cobb made himself a good hitter. Jackson was born a good hitter."

Jackson had some curious encounters against Hubert "Dutch" Leonard, a left-hander who began in the majors with the Red Sox in 1913 and ended his career with the Tigers in 1925. But his opportunities to come up against Leonard were limited. At the start of his career the pitcher was so frustrated pitching to Jackson that he once entered a game declaring that he would knock him down each time he came to bat. In Jackson's first at bat, Leonard fired a pitch that cracked Jackson behind the neck. The next time a Leonard pitch slammed into Jackson's ribs. Coming to bat for the third time in the game, Jackson was hit in the head by a Leonard pitch. The ball caromed off his baseball cap and bounced into the stands. Jackson staggered down to first base.

"I caught that game," recalled Larry Woodall, former Detroit backstop. "Jackson was so innocent and free from guile that he said to Leonard while going down to first: 'I never knew you to be so wild before.' Joe just didn't realize that Dutch was throwing at him."

The wild ones, the wily ones, the control artists, the legends, all were fair game for Joe Jackson and his whiplash swing.

JOE JACKSON: "All the left-handers I ever saw were suckers. I never could understand why left-handed batters complained that they couldn't hit left-handed pitchers. You needed just nerve out there. . . . I used to laugh at the pitchers and it would make them mad. Once Huggins told Waite Hoyt to walk me and I kidded Hoyt. He lost his temper and threw one that just grazed my ankles. I hit it into the stands. I used to get Coveleski crazy. I said 'Just throw that ball anywhere near me, Polack, and they will have to pick it out of your throat!' "

TRIS SPEAKER: "Jackson was not only a natural hitter, but he had a set style, a grooved swing. I can't remember that he was ever in a batting slump. His swing was so perfect there was little chance of it ever getting disorganized. He was the greatest natural hitter who ever lived."

As a fielder, there were also very few better than Jackson. It was said that he could throw a ball 350 feet with speed and accuracy. After catching the third out in left field he would sometimes trot to the wall, turn, and throw the ball over the home-plate backdrop—more than 400 feet.

In 1917, a charity All Star Game in Boston, the Tim Murane benefit exhibition, was staged. The game was preceded by a field meet and a throwing contest.

JOE JACKSON: "I didn't even know I was in it. Cobb and Speaker slipped around and entered me. I was sittin' out by the flagpole and when they called my name, I just picked up a ball and throwed it to home plate and that was the winning throw."

The throw was 396 feet, eight inches. The next-best throw was a tie—Duffy Lewis of Boston and Clarence (Tillie) Walker of the Philadelphia Athletics both reached 384 feet, six inches.

For the effort Jackson received a big silver bowl inscribed "Won by Joe Jackson of the White Sox, the World's Greatest Slugger, for throwing a baseball farther than any of the stars . . ."

JOE JACKSON: "When the All Star Game started, it was a 10-to-1 shot we'd beat 'em to death. I thought we had the prettiest ball club I ever did see stacked together."

The American League outfield was Tris Speaker, Ty Cobb, and Jackson, Stuffy Mcinnis and George Sisler at first base, and Eddie Collins at second. Buck Weaver played third base and Boston's Everett Scott was at shortstop. Walter Johnson was the American League's starting pitcher. But the Nationals, on a double by Rabbit Maranville, won the game.

On August 19, 1917, the first Sunday baseball game was played in the Polo Grounds in New York City. Managers John McGraw of the Giants and his former star pitcher, Christy Mathewson of the Reds, who had never performed on a Sunday when he was an active player, were arrested for violating a New York City law that banned baseball on Sunday.

On September 2 and 3, Chicago won a pair of back-to-back doubleheaders from the Tigers. Later charges would surface that Detroit "lay down" and that a pool was collected among the White Sox players to reward the Tigers for their non-efforts. The charges were never proven. But the twin doubleheader sweep triggered a Chicago breakaway to the pennant. On September 21 in Boston, Red Faber was tabbed to pitch the pennant clincher. He faced Babe Ruth with the bases loaded and got him to hit into a game-ending double play. Faber had his sixteenth win, and the White Sox wound up finishing the season nine games ahead of Boston.

Before a game that September Jackson shared a few quiet moments with an old adversary: thirty-seven-year-old Sam Crawford, in his nineteenth and final major league season. Crawford retired from the majors with a record 312 career triples and 50 inside-the-park home runs. He would play on for a couple of more seasons in the Pacific Coast League.

Nagging injuries that 1917 season saw Jackson bat .301, his career low. But the White Sox won the pennant, recording the best winning percentage in the club's history by winning 100 of the 154 games they played. They were virtually unbeatable at Comiskey Park: 57 wins and just 20 losses gave them a .740 percentage. They led the league in stolen bases, triples, and runs scored. "Pants" Rowland became the first manager with no major league playing experience to win a pennant.

Ambivalent work ethics, factionalism, divided loyalties, cliques, and outright hostility between teammates, characterized some of the major league teams of that time. There were cliques of college players that included Christy Mathewson, Harry Hooper, Eddie Collins, Jack Coombs, Frank Chance, Chief Meyers, Ed Reulbach, Eddie Plank, and Art Devlin. There were factions based on sectionalism—city slickers versus farm boys like Joe Jackson. There were schisms springing from ethnic background. There were problems stemming from disproportionate salaries. Nowhere was this more evident than on the Chicago White Sox.

Debonair Eddie Collins was so disliked by many of the players on the White Sox that none of the other infielders threw the ball to him during warmups; Collins had to settle for Ray Schalk to play catch with. Risberg harbored a special dislike for Collins, begrudging him his high salary, talent, education, good character, and gentlemanliness. Buck Weaver was even more hostile, often criticizing Collins for never sharpening his spikes.

BUCK WEAVER: "He figures they might come back at him and he'd get hurt playing there in the infield. He was a great guy to look out for himself. If there was a tough gent coming down to second, he'd yell for the shortstop to take the ball."

Yet, despite their interpersonal problems, their prejudices against one another, their private vanities and petty jealousies, the 1917 White Sox of Chicago were a solid team, a group of men that played an exciting brand of baseball, a team appreciated by the fans.

Charles A. Comiskey appreciated them, too. Hungering for the first White Sox pennant in the dozen years since the time of the "Hitless Wonders," he had promised all of his players a bonus if they won the flag. And he kept his word. A case of cheap champagne was their bonus.

RING LARDNER: "It tasted like stale piss."

The New York Giants and their feisty manager John J. McGraw were the competition for the White Sox in the World Series. The man they called "Mugsy" had a notorious past. In 1902, McGraw had arrived in New York on July 7. He had been released or relieved—depending on who is telling the story—as manager by the Baltimore Orioles, who owed him $7,000, a loan he had made to cover club debts. McGraw brought along some help with him to the Giants in the battery of "Iron Man" Joe McGinnity and catcher Roger Bresnahan. Stripped of these three and others, the Orioles were unable to field a team for a game against St. Louis on July 17. An infuriated Ban Johnson restocked Baltimore and kept that team and his league alive.

For John McGraw, the World Series against the White Sox was a holy war between the National League and the American League.

Prior to the series Charles Comiskey garnered headlines by announcing that he would donate one percent of Chicago's World Series shares to Clark Griffith's Bat and Ball Fund for American soldiers in France.

During the 1917 season the White Sox had attracted special attention all around the American League when they were on the road. The team had given up its gray road uniforms and worn a kind of reverse pinstripe—white stripes on a dark blue fabric with matching caps. For the World Series Comiskey ordered up a uniform that was even more unique. The Sox wore a specially created spangled red-white-and-blue uniform. Even the white stockings were given red-and-blue designer stripes. "Gaudy" was the word most fans used to describe the uniform that had a one-time use in the 1917 Series and was then retired.

A seven-hitter by Eddie Cicotte, who that season at the age of thirty-three had won twenty-eight games and posted a 1.53 ERA, gave Chicago a 2–1 home victory in Game One on October 6. A home run by Felsch in the fourth inning off Slim Sallee was the game's decisive hit.

In Game Two a five-run fourth inning on six singles gave the Sox a 7–2 win. Red Faber outdueled four New York pitchers to notch the win for Chicago. He also revealed the lack of communication on the White Sox when he attempted to steal third base in the fifth inning. Buck Weaver was on third at the time.

The series shifted to the Polo Grounds for the next two games. Rube Benton became the first left-hander to pitch a World Series shutout, beating Cicotte 2–0 in Game Three. Then Ferdie Schupp, 21–7 during the regular season with a 1.95 ERA, fanned seven and shut out Chicago, 5–0, to tie the series. In that game Benny Kauff smacked two home runs, one an inside-the-park drive to deep center field.

The fifth game back in Chicago saw the teams combine for a total of 26 hits and nine errors as the White Sox won 8–5. The good news for the White Sox in that game was the gutsy relief pitching of Cicotte, who came in for Reb Russell in the first inning and pitched six strong innings, giving up just two runs. Eddie Collins singled in the go-ahead run in a three-run eighth.

Game Six took place in New York on October 15 before 33,969, the biggest crowd of the Series. Red Faber and Rube Benton hurled three scoreless innings each. Then, in the fourth, Eddie Collins wound up on second base after hitting a ground ball to third that Heinie Zimmerman threw past first baseman Walter Holke. Jackson lofted a fly ball to right. The ball was dropped by Dave Robertson. Collins moved to third base. Felsch then tapped one back to Benton. Collins headed home. Benton threw to Zimmerman at third, and Collins kept running. Catcher Rariden came up to help get Collins in the rundown, but he came up too close. Collins spun past him before Zimmerman could throw the ball. All the frustrated Zimmerman could do was chase Collins all the way across home plate. Later, when he was criticized, Zimmerman snapped, "Who the hell was I going to throw the ball to—umpire Bill Klem?" A single by Gandil then scored Jackson and Felsch.

JOE JACKSON: "That game gave me one of my biggest thrills, I guess, in baseball. That was the game when Heinie Zimmerman chased Eddie Collins across the plate with the tying run and then, with me and Felsch on base, Gandil hit for two bases scoring us and we win the ballgame 4–2 and the Series."

The 1917 World Series performance of Joe Jackson was good but not sensational. He collected 7 hits in 23 tries, a .304 clip, scored four runs, drove in two runs, and stole a base.

On October 16, a day after the World Series, in Garden City, Long Island, the Giants and the White Sox met in an exhibition game before 600 soldiers. Chicago won the game, 6–4.

That offseason of 1917 the main news was the death and destruction in Europe, the ravages of World War I. The nation's music reflected the time with such titles as "I Didn't Raise My Son to be a Soldier," "Over There," "Smiles," "Goodbye Broadway, Hello France," and "I'm Always Chasing Rainbows." And so did sporting goods catalogs. The Partridge Company issued a catalog depicting Rube Marquard in Uncle Sam's uniform at bat with the headline: BATTER UP—UNCLE SAM IS AT THE PLATE.

By the end of the Great War 550 men who had or would play major league baseball had served in the Armed Forces. That figure included 124 players from the American League and 103 from the National League. Several, like A.T. Burr and Eddie Grant (who was killed in action in the Argonne Forest) were just a part of the 50,000 American dead and 200,000 wounded.

The Sox began 1918 in a snakebitten mode, and they continued that way. The train carrying the team to spring training derailed near Weatherford, Texas, on March 18. Miraculously no one was injured. A couple of days later Jackson was in a friend's touring car along with Schalk, Cicotte, and Gandil.

They were returning from a golf course. Another car plowed into them. Again, all the players escaped injury. The only problem was whiplash sustained by Cicotte.

CHARLES COMISKEY: "Their place was on the ball field, not out experimenting with golf sticks and looking at scenery."

At first there were fears that the 1918 season would not be allowed to get under way. But a compromise was worked out that cut the schedule to 140 games and mandated that the World Series would start on September 5. Roster player limits were abolished to accommodate losses to the draft. Most teams also cut players' salaries because of what the owners claimed were the demands of war. Connie Mack told his players that they should trust him and take a chance on their salaries. Profit sharing, he called it. "If we make ten thousand," Mack said, "we will gladly share it with them."

The federal government created a special 10 percent entertainment tax on admission that was applicable to any "rented space." Even those who watched games from rooftops adjoining ballparks were not immune from the tax, which impacted on ticket prices at Comiskey Park. In 1918, a bleacher seat was priced at thirty cents, grandstand admission was raised to fifty-five cents, and box seats were $1.10.

The season got under way. Then, on May 23, a government order deemed baseball nonessential to the war effort, and a "work or fight" edict was issued, giving eligible major league draftees the choice of entering the service or working for wartime industries. The New York Giants were hit hard by losses as Kauff, Benton, and Jeff Tesreau were lost to the draft-or-defense work.

Schisms on the White Sox widened. Some players, like Eddie Collins and Red Faber, went off to the Armed Forces. Others, like Lefty Williams, who only pitched in fifteen games for the Sox and Joe Jackson, who played in just seventeen games and was slugging the ball at a .354 pace for the 1918 White Sox, opted for wartime industry. Jackson made his decision after his draft board in Greenville reversed its Class-4 designation and advanced him to Class-1—eligible for military service.

Jackson was, at age thirty, the sole support for his wife Katie, his mother, and a brother. He felt he had been treated unfairly by the political power structure. But he said nothing and just did what many other players did—accepted the choice offered by the government order—employment in wartime industry.

Jackson worked in the shipyards and played in a "patriotic baseball league" for the Harlan and Hollingsworth Shipbuilding Company, a subsidiary of Bethlehem Steel located in Wilmington, Delaware. Players who followed Jackson's course and others who managed to play in the majors while the war raged were scorned as slackers.

Curiously, however, it was Joe Jackson who was most on the cutting edge, the one major leaguer who received the bulk of the bad press. A newspaper account of May 16 reported:

> Either the fighting blood of the Jacksons is not as red
> as it used to be in the days of Old Stonewall and Old
> Hickory or 'General Joe' of the Chicago White Sox
> concluded there was enough of the family in the war
> alrcady . . .with four brothers in service, he has indicated
> that he will flee to the refuge of a shipyard hoping thus to
> escape service. Probably Mrs. Jackson who is the boss of
> the family has had some influences also in her husband's
> determination to take up ship building in preference to
> trench work.

The *New York Herald* reported that he had "conscientious objections to getting hurt in defense of his country and to associating with patriots."

A *Chicago Tribune* editorial particularly took him to task, characterizing Jackson as a person of "unusual physical development, and presumably [he] would make an excellent fighting man, but it appears that Mr. Jackson would prefer not to fight." The diatribe ended with the words: "Good Americans will not be very enthusiastic over seeing him play baseball after the war is over."

Even American League president Ban Johnson got into the act: "I hope that the provost marshall yanks Jackson and these other evaders from the shipyards and the steel works by the coat collar. I hope they are sent to cantonments to prepare for future events on the western front."

Major league club owners were especially piqued by the movement of their players into industrial league baseball. They viewed the moves as a not-too-subtle skirting of the reserve clause, their legal tool that gave them total power over players. Comiskey, one of the owners so angered by the state of affairs, snapped that when the war was concluded there would be "no room for the jumpers" on his team.

CHARLES COMISKEY: "I don't consider them fit to play for my club. I hate to see any players, particularly my own, go to the shipyards to escape service."

In 1918, Mississippi became the last state to pass a compulsory education law. That summer United States soldiers and sailors played exhibition baseball games before King George of Great Britain. The Somme, Armentieres, Trading with the Enemy Act, Doughboys—new terms like these evoked images of war.

Boston manager Jack Barry was drafted, and executive Ed Barrow took over the Red Sox. He decided to have Babe Ruth play the outfield between starts. It was a decision that would have a profound effect on baseball history. The Babe won thirteen games as a pitcher; as a batter he hit .300 and led the league with eleven home runs, the first of his dozen home run titles.

Without Jackson, Faber, Collins, Risberg, Felsch, and Williams, all gone for most of the year in the service or wartime industry, the White Sox hovered around the .500 level until about the middle of June. Then the team fell apart.

The abbreviated baseball schedule created some statistical oddities. Sherry Magee led the National League in RBIs with just 76, and no senior-circuit pitcher worked more than 300 innings. The only bit of normalcy was Ty Cobb's performance. He won another batting title, this time with a .382 average.

The negative publicity about able-bodied athletes avoiding military service and a shortened schedule of 128 games made the 1918 season the biggest financial flop of the ragtime era. The White Sox drew just 195,081 fans, down from 684,521 the year before. Their record dropped to 57–67 from the 100–54 of 1917. They finished in sixth place, seventeen games behind the Boston Red Sox, who faced off on September 5 against the other Chicago team, the Cubs, in the World Series. Ironically, the home park for the postseason event for the Cubs was Comiskey Park. The Cubs abandoned their North Side ballpark and agreed to play at Comiskey Park, a much larger facility, with hopes of bigger gate receipts.

The owners were criticized for even scheduling a World Series in wartime, when so many players had gone off to France. With wartime travel restraints in operation, the World Series had just one scheduled shift for travel after the third game.

With Boston leading in the series three games to one, players feared that they would not receive their World Series shares. The rules of the Series payout had been changed, with payments made instead to the top four finishers in each league. Harry Hooper led a delegation of four players to meet with the National Commission, the ruling body of baseball, before the game the next day. Hooper, the right fielder on Boston's fabled George "Duffy" Lewis-Tris Speaker-Hooper outfield, was one of the more respected players of the era. But even he could not obtain satisfaction from the power structure that the players would be rightfully compensated.

Game Five was about to begin that afternoon in Boston. There was a restlessness in the crowd of nearly 30,000. No players had taken the field. It was the second "strike" in baseball history. The first one was in 1912, a one-game walkout by the Detroit Tigers.

American League President Ban Johnson, a drinking man, was in high spirits when he met with Cubs spokesmen Harry Hooper and Leslie Mann just before the game. Ignoring Mann,

Johnson turned his attention to Hooper. "Harry, do you realize you are a member of one of the greatest organizations in the world, the American League? And do you realize what you will do to its good name if you do not play? Go out there, Harry, the crowd is waiting for you." Then Boston Mayor Fitzgerald also intervened, using the war effort as a goad to convince the men to play.

Taking the field almost an hour late, the Red Sox and Cubs played the game. Boston lost that day but clinched the title a day later on a three-hitter by Carl Mays, his second win of the Series. Babe Ruth posted the other two wins as a pitcher for the Sox.

The expected winner's share of $2,000 became $890 per player, and the loser's expected share of $1,400 was $535. War taxes, it was said, and other deductions were factored in. It was just another case of owners shortchanging players—a practice most of the moguls had a lot of experience in and at which they were quite proficient. And it was said that no one did it better than Charles Albert Comiskey.

5

1919

In 1919, the "war to end all wars" was over. More than 50,000 young American soldiers had died in action and more than 200,000 were wounded. There were new heroes with names like Sergeant Alvin York, Black Jack Pershing, and Captain Eddie Rickenbacker. And a war-weary nation returned to peaceful pursuits.

Grover Cleveland Alexander had come back from France, deaf in one ear because of exposure to severe shelling. In 1919 he would win sixteen games—nine of them shutouts—and lead the National League in ERA. But epilepsy and alcoholism were ready to seize control and haunt him the rest of his days. It was a season when Ty Cobb would bat .384 and win his final batting title, when Babe Ruth would set a new slugging percentage record of .657 and a new home run record with 29, breaking the major league record of 27 set in 1884 by Ned Williamson.

In New York City, Sunday baseball was legalized. National League rosters were cut from twenty-five to twenty-three players. American League rosters were reduced to twenty-one players. Both leagues moved to save money. Owners reduced scheduled games to 140 from the usual 154. Their reasoning was that there would be lessened interest in baseball. But the very opposite was the case, as fans sickened by the war sought escape through baseball.

Many experts felt the White Sox of Chicago were the best

team in baseball, and one of the best of all time. Although the *Chicago Tribune* had picked them to finish third, a sense of high optimism pervaded their ranks as they readied themselves for the long season. The team was essentially the same one that had won it all in 1917.

CHARLES COMISKEY: "It's the best bunch of fighters I ever saw. It's a wonderful combo, the greatest team I ever had."

On the road, the White Sox were an attractive aggregation. They drew the largest crowds in baseball during that era, even larger than McGraw's New York Giants. At home their loyal and knowledgeable fans came out in record numbers to watch them play ball. Even late-summer race riots in Chicago would not diminish the enthusiasm of their supporters.

Charles Comiskey continued to glory in his nickname, "the Noblest Roman of Them All," a reference to his aquiline nose and the public perception of his alleged generosity. In truth, his image and nickname belied reality. He alone decided how much each player on his team was paid. The amount was subject neither to discussion nor appeal. A classic example of Comiskey's niggardliness concerned Hall of Famer Ed Walsh, a forty-game-winner one season. Walsh was rewarded with a salary of $3,200.

The White Sox salaries were among the lowest in the sport. The 1919 White Sox payroll topped out at $85,000. A few years later Babe Ruth would earn that much by himself. Except for Eddie Collins, who earned $15,000—a little more than the combined salaries of Felsch, Gandil, and Jackson—all the White Sox players were grossly underpaid.

Joe Jackson earned only $6,000. Eddie Cicotte, thirty-five, the ace of the pitching staff, a player who was 28–12 in 1917, earned $500 less than Jackson. Perhaps the best pitcher in the league next to Walter Johnson, Cicotte was called the master of the shineball.

EDDIE CICOTTE: "Oh, heck that wasn't any shine-ball. One day in New York the Yankees asked, 'What is that froggie going to throw us today?' And our guys said, 'Wait until you see this one, this shine-ball.' But I didn't put paraffin on it like the newspapers said. I used to rub it on my pants but it was shiny already. I didn't have anything on my pants but sweat. But Ban Johnson, he called me in five times and he said, 'You better cut that out.' I would say, "Cut what out?' He would say, "Never mind what. Just cut it out.' One day in Cleveland when I got through, two detectives grabbed my pants and Johnson sent them to a laboratory looking for paraffin. I pitched with a curve and a riser—I could throw the ball through a curtain ring all afternoon."

Pitcher Lefty Williams was referred to as "the biggest and littlest man in baseball" because he had a burly neck and shoulders but a small body. His salary was just $2,600. Newly acquired pitcher Dickie Kerr, a soft-spoken Texan, earned under $3,000. Swede Risberg, who said he quit school in the third grade in San Francisco because he "refused to shave," was paid $3,250.

Clarence "Pants" Rowland was no longer the manager of the White Sox. The scapegoat for Chicago's failure in 1918, Rowland was fired by Comiskey and replaced by William "Kid" Gleason. A former pitcher and second baseman, the fifty-two-year-old Gleason's nickname derived from his enthusiasm for the game and his small physical stature. He was barely over 5'6".

JOHN McGRAW: "He was, without doubt, the gamest and most spirited ballplayer I ever saw and that doesn't except Ty Cobb. He was a great influence for good on any ball club, making up for his lack of stature by his spirit and fight."

One of Gleason's first managerial decisions was to appoint Eddie Collins team captain. Gleason harbored no special affection for Collins, but he knew that class and intelligence won out in crucial situations on the playing field. Collins would run the team out on the field.

Gleason had been a coach for the White Sox for a half a dozen seasons, and Joe Jackson respected him.

CONNIE MACK: "I guess that Kid Gleason knew how to handle him. The Kid was a rough, tough fellow who would fight his weight in wildcats and a man like Jackson couldn't help but toe the mark when Kid said the word. The Kid thought the world of the big fellow, too."

Spring training in 1919 did not begin until late March. The owners delayed its start as an additional cost-saving device. Joe Jackson had hit very well in the shipyard leagues in 1918 and reported in good condition to spring training. There he used his time wisely to further condition his already lean body. As spring training neared its conclusion Jackson felt fully primed to have a big year. But he was very concerned about the reception he would receive when the season opened. Though there were many ballplayers in the Armed Forces in World War I, lots of them had been placed in Special Services. There they did nothing but play ball, but they escaped the degree of criticism Jackson suffered. Fearing he would be a magnet for abuse and because of the charges of being a slacker, he readied himself for Opening Day of the 1919 season in Chicago.

Jackson was ready for anything, but he was quite unprepared for what happened. When he came to the plate for his first at bat, the game was halted for a moment while a delegation of his most loyal fans presented him with a glistening gold pocket watch. In later years he would carefully finger the watch and remember that moment. All through the game about four hundred fans, "Jackson Rooters" they called themselves, milled about and marched behind a booming big brass band.

Each time Joe Jackson stepped up to the plate, "Give 'em Black Betsy, Joe! Give 'em Black Betsy!" rang out. In the fifth inning a big bedsheet was draped along the railing of the right-field boxes. Printed in big black letters were the words JACKSON ROOTERS.

That season, Joe Jackson honed in on his game and himself. At age thirty, a ten-year veteran, he had already borne his share of ragging—the charges early on that he was a coward, the ribbing about his illiteracy, and the slacker charges that he still heard from time to time. He was content to swing Black Betsy, to hit the blue darters, to keep his batting average well above .300. Of course, he heard his teammates whining and complaining in the clubhouse. He listened to the cursing on the trains. He shied away from it all. There was also the midseason aborted plan for a strike aimed at getting salary increases. He would have no part of that, either.

Through that long season he found serenity in quiet moments with Katie. They had no children and would have none, but they had a good marriage, a strong bond to each other. He would tell her about the common types on the team, the hostility, and the fact that the White Sox were split into factions, in Jackson's words "split up into two gangs."

One side was led by aristocratic Eddie Collins. The other was headed up by coarse Chick Gandil. The Collins faction included Schalk, Shano Collins, Red Faber, Dickie Kerr, and Nemo Leibold. Gandil's group was an aggregation of the less educated, more earthy players: Swede Risberg, Lefty Williams, Buck Weaver, Happy Felsch, Eddie Cicotte, and Fred McMullin, a reserve infielder. Education and geography placed Jackson in this camp. Off the field there was little cooperation or communication between the two camps. Some players didn't talk to others; very few spoke to Gandil or Felsch. Yet, somehow on the field they worked together like a fine-tuned machine.

On May 30, the White Sox were in first place with a four-game lead. But the lead didn't last for long. Through the blazing days of summer they traded places up at the top of the American League with Cleveland and the emerging powerhouse New York Yankees.

On June 14 workhorse Eddie Cicotte defeated the Athletics for the twelfth straight time. On June 23 Happy Felsch tied a record with twelve chances in a nine-inning game. On August 14, his four assists in the outfield would tie another major league record.

Around the circuit through the dog days of summer the White Sox of Chicago played their games. The heart of their batting order—Buck Weaver, third; Joe Jackson, cleanup; and Happy Felsch, fifth—pounded the ball steadily, a nightmare trio for opposing pitchers. But despite the collective skills of the Chicago players, the pennant race was a tough one.

On September 10, the American League's only no-hitter

that season was pitched by Cleveland southpaw Ray Coveleski. He baffled the Yankees, 3–0. Just a couple of weeks before, Coveleski had been struck by lightning and knocked unconscious. There were those who said his no-hitter was charged with high voltage. Coveleski's no-hitter triggered a ten-game Cleveland winning streak. The Indians wound up winning thirteen of their final seventeen games, but their final spurt saw them fall short.

On September 24 a 6–5 Chicago win over St. Louis clinched the pennant for the White Sox. Joe Jackson's ninth-inning blue darter drove in the winning run. The White Sox finished the season 3½ games ahead of Cleveland.

It had been a great season for major league baseball. Overall attendance for 1919 was 6.5 million, up dramatically from the 3 million of the year before. Some teams tripled their attendance figures of 1918, and even the weakest of teams like the Phillies, Cardinals, Braves, and Senators finished in the black.

On paper the White Sox of Chicago were hands down baseball's best team. Their team batting average of .287 and their 668 runs scored were tops in the majors. The siege gun for their attack was Joe Jackson, who missed just one game in 1919 and batted .351, fourth in the league behind Cobb, Bobby Veach, and George Sisler. He was also third in hits and RBIs, fourth in total bases and triples, fifth in slugging percentage, and the club leader in home runs.

The Sox had tremendous defense from catcher Ray Schalk, shortstop Swede Risberg, center fielder Happy Felsch, who led all American League outfielders in assists, second baseman Eddie Collins, who batted .319, and third baseman Buck Weaver. Twenty-nine-year-old Fred McMullin batted .294 and was a valued reserve.

The pitching staff lacked quantity but made up for it in quality starters. Workhorse Eddie Cicotte led the league in wins (29), complete games (30), and innings pitched (307). Control pitcher Lefty Williams posted a 23–11 record and led the American League in games started with 40. Rookie Dickie Kerr won 13 games, and Red Faber won 11 but would see no action in the World Series because of injuries. Comiskey knew his team would need Dickie Kerr at the top of his form in the World Series against Cincinnati.

The Reds were managed by Pat Moran, known affectionately to the Cincinnati fans as "Dot Irisher" and not so affectionately to National League bench jockeys as "Old Whiskey Face." A native of Fitchburg, Massachusetts, Moran had been hired on January 30, 1919, when there was no word about the whereabouts of manager Christy Mathewson, still in France.

The Reds were a solid but not a sensational team. On July 6, they swept a doubleheader from the Pirates and took over first place. They were in and out of the National League's top spot throughout July. In August, they clamped down on their hold on first and finally pulled away from the pack. They wound up winning the National League pennant by nine games. The pennant victory now had fans referring to Moran as "Miracle Man." The one legitimate star on the Reds was center fielder Edd Roush, whose .321 batting average led the National League.

EDD ROUSH: "One of my chores was to milk the cows, which meant getting up before dawn and going out to that cold dark barn. I didn't expect to make it all the way to the big leagues. I just had to get away from those damn cows."

Cincinnati also had Jake Daubert, a solid performer at first base, and third baseman Heinie Groh, who batted .310 in 1919. They had a lot of good pitching: left-handers Slim Sallee (21–7), and Dutch Ruether (19–6), and right-handers Hod Eller (20–9), Jimmy Ring, Ray Fisher, and Havana-born Dolf Luque.

It was with a great sense of anticipation that baseball fans, especially those in the Midwest, looked forward to the 1919 World Series—a matchup of the underdog Cincinnati Reds and the powerful Chicago White Sox.

The ten-cent World Series preview issue of *The Sporting News* featured a team picture of the Reds with a seven-column headline: JOY IF REDS WIN—BUT A SHOCK IF THEY DO. Lesser headlines proclaimed SENTIMENT PICKS MORANMEN, BUT JUDGMENT PICKS SOX. And THOROUGH OPINIONS OF MOST CRITICS IS NOTED

THREAD OF CONVICTION THAT GLEASON HEADS TEAM THAT CARRIES A
CLASS NOT POSSESSED BY NATIONAL LEAGUE RIVAL.

As if knowing that the 1919 World Series would be of special and supreme importance to him, Joe Jackson intensified his fetish of collecting hairpins. He looked everywhere for them. He also extended the time he spent sitting alone in a dark room staring with one eye closed at a lit candle. Not really able to put how he felt into words, Joe nevertheless sensed there was something magical and mystical about the process. The one closed eye, the other open wide and burning into the luminous light—the ritual was for Jackson not only a means of strengthening his vision but a conduit toward better mental focus, a passage for relief from the stress of the moment. He also felt the eye exercises made his vision keener and were a reason why he was such a tough strikeout. Jackson struck out just once every twenty-five at bats throughout his career.

The first two games of the World Series were scheduled for Cincinnati. Redland Field was the home of the Reds. When it had been formally dedicated on May 18, 1912, Ban Johnson, previously a Cincinnati sportswriter, and Charles Comiskey, who managed the Reds in the 1890s, were present. Now they were on hand in vastly different roles.

The Cincinnati ballpark, unlike some others, had clubhouses for visiting and home players. That was a relief for the visiting White Sox who, throughout most of their travels, steeled themselves for the rides on public transportation while dressed in full uniform. At least performing at Redland Field they would not have to worry about how they would dodge mudballs thrown at them on their way to the park by some of the more brazen youth.

The park's dimensions were spacious—360 feet down the lines and 420 feet to dead center field. Single-deck pavilions stretched along the outfield foul lines. Right field contained a bleacher section. There was a wooden scoreboard and a primitive public address system created from more than a dozen loudspeaker horns. A flagpole rose eighty-two feet above the playing surface, although any ball striking it remained in play.

The Redland Field flagpole was actually the third tallest "in play" structure in baseball history. Only the flagpole in Tiger Stadium in Detroit and the left-field light tower in Grayson Stadium in Savannah were taller. Joe Jackson, interestingly enough, was one of the few players in history able to take aim at all three of them.

A few days before the start of the best-of-nine series the White Sox were a 3–1 betting favorite. To everyone the odds were on target. The American League had won eight of the last nine series; position for position the vaunted White Sox had the edge on the Reds.

But suddenly huge amounts of money began to appear, put up by bettors who favored Cincinnati. Big time New York gambler Arnold Rothstein allegedly was behind a lot of the money swing to the Reds. Actually, it was more than a swing—it was closer to a hurricane.

Sportswriter Hugh Fullerton, who had obtained his first job in journalism through the efforts of Charles Comiskey and was friendly with the Chicago owner, told some of his sportswriter friends, "Every dog in the streets knows it smells. Keep your eyes open. A lot of strange things may happen before this series ends."

A lot of strange things had already happened in baseball throughout its rather brief history. In the National League's initial season of 1876, the Brooklyn Mutuals and the Philadelphia Athletics had dropped out before the season ended. They were unable to make the final western swing because of financial problems. That spared baseball from a lot of messy headlines, because league president Morgan G. Bulkeley was set to expel both teams for throwing a game.

In 1877, four Louisville players sent telegrams to gamblers that contained the code word "SASH," which meant "sure as shit" the fix was on. Those four players were banned for life.

Through baseball pools thousands of dollars changed hands weekly during the ragtime era. A fan could purchase a pool ticket for as little as ten cents and then win by selecting the team that won the most games, scored the most runs, and so on, in a specific week. The managers of the pools had the cooperation of the newspapers, who published the betting line on games and ran weekly statistics on hits, runs, etc. The climate for gambling was always sunny.

At one time there was a ban on any public announcement of who the starting pitchers would be for a given game for fear hurlers would be approached by gamblers. There were instances where outfielders poised to catch a ball would have rocks thrown at them by fans. The rocks were not thrown in anger, but as a distraction to the play by those who had something to gain financially if the catch were not made. More extreme instances also took place. Once a gambler charged onto the field and tackled a player to prevent a play. Another time a sharpshooter with a gun pelted the ground around a player who was chasing down a long line drive.

Players placed bets on themselves and their teams. Even the legendary Walter Johnson and the great Ty Cobb were involved in this practice. Various owners, managers, and players had intimate links with underworld figures. New York Giants manager John J. McGraw spent a lot of his time with gamblers, owned a part interest in two race tracks, and had a passion for playing the horses.

In the first World Series, in 1903, catcher Lou Criger allegedly walked away from a $12,000 bribe. In the second World Series, gamblers offered Rube Waddell $17,000 not to show up. He didn't, but he couldn't, injured as he was from tripping over a suitcase.

In 1908, some highly irate Phillies players threw a gambler down a flight of stairs from the clubhouse at the Polo Grounds. In a series in 1916, the New York Giants reportedly played with little verve to enable the Dodgers to beat out the Phillies for the pennant.

Hal Chase was a skilled first baseman with a great deal of style. Fans loved to see him charge in on the batter, scoop up the ball, and make plays at any base. But those inside the world of baseball spoke about his "corkscrew mind." New York manager George Stallings accused Chase of throwing a game in

1910. Using that "corkscrew mind" to his advantage, Chase survived the charge and even wound up taking Stallings' job. In 1918, then with Cincinnati, Chase was accused in several court affidavits of tampering with games. One affidavit presented by manager Christy Mathewson and owner Garry Hermann of the Cincinnati Reds contained a letter from pitcher Mike Regan. It told of an offer made to him by Chase in Boston in 1918 that carried a $200 price tag. It was tied to Regan pitching to win or lose as Chase instructed. Regan refused the offer. Another affidavit by Reds right fielder Greasy Neale claimed that Chase had bragged that he had won $500 after the Reds were swept in a doubleheader in Philadelphia. Neale also described how Chase told him at another time to bet $200 on the Reds because "this is the day for the Reds to win."

William D. (Pol) Perritt, a pitcher on the New York Giants, swore in an affidavit that Chase approached him before the Giants' final visit to Cincinnati in 1918 and inquired as to which game Perritt was going to work. "You needn't be afraid of me," Chase told Perritt. The pitcher told John McGraw what had happened and the Giants manager said, "The players ought to drive Chase from baseball." McGraw corroborated that conversation in an affidavit, noting that he had observed Perritt engaged in lengthy conversation with Chase.

It was a customary practice during the ragtime era and even before for a contender to offer a suit of clothes as a reward to a pitcher on a non-contending team who defeated a contending team. In 1917 the appreciative White Sox, presented new suits to Detroit players who lost two doubleheaders.

There was a lot of damnable evidence against players and managers throughout the ragtime era. But no action was ever taken in response to any charges of gambling by the National Commission, the ruling body of baseball. A cover-up of all reports was the order of the day.

Despite the fact that baseball, since its inception had been tied to gambling, with constant rumors of fixed games and other irregularities, what Fullerton was intimating seemed pure balderdash. And most of those who heard his remarks dismissed them as the words of an iconoclast, the bluster and boasting of a man who liked to startle others.

A World Series being fixed? How can you fix eighteen men? The World Series was America's premier sporting event, the glamorous, the crowning culmination of a long season. It was ceremony and ritual intertwined—the best versus the best. The World Series being fixed? The thought boggled the imagination, defied the odds, conjured up fantasies. . . .

On the final road trip of the 1919 season, the White Sox were in Boston. Joe Jackson was out enjoying the New England air in Kenmore Square, in the shadow of Fenway Park. Chick Gandil approached him. After a few pleasantries were passed, Gandil snapped out, "Seven of us have gotten together to frame up the World Series. You'll get $10,000 if you help us out."

Jackson was taken aback. But he recovered and said, "No, I want no part of that." Gandil persisted. Jackson turned down the offer again and walked away.

A few days later in Chicago, Gandil again approached him. This time the ante was raised to $20,000. "Joe," Gandil said, "it's going to happen with you or without you. You don't have to do much." Again Jackson refused, but the two offers had upset him. And though he had declined to be part of any plot, he felt a bit like an apple poised to be thrown into a barrel of rotten ones.

JOE JACKSON: "I never said anything about it until the night before the Series started. I went to Mr. Comiskey and begged him to take me out of the lineup. . . . If there was something going on I knew the bench would be the safest place, but he wouldn't listen to me. . . ."

6

World Series

On October 1, 1919, an unseasonably hot fall day, both teams came out under blue skies to take batting practice at oddly shaped Redland Field in Cincinnati. Unbelievably, the betting odds were now even money. Outside the park, scalpers were elated. They were asking for and getting as much as twenty-five dollars a ticket—a previously unheard of price.

Jack Doyle, owner of the Billiard Academy in New York City, a famed betting center of the time, said, "You couldn't miss it . . . The thing had an odor. I saw smart guys take even money on the Sox who should have been asking 5 to 1."

Ed Bang was one of a hundred members of an expanded press corps who covered the World Series.

ED BANG: "I recall vividly the late [sportswriter] Ed P. Strong phoned me at the LaSalle Hotel before the first game and told me he had a great story for me. He couldn't discuss the matter over the phone but came to my hotel room and gave me the information about the scandal. He named eight players and concluded with 'and they are taking poor Joe Jackson for a ride.' In other words Ed conveyed to me the easygoing Jackson didn't know what it was all about. I have always believed that because I never knew Joe to have even an off-color thought . . . of conniving to blacken the name of baseball which had been good to him."

In the stands, vendors were hawking the Cincinnati Golden Jubilee World Series program for twenty-five cents each. The sixteenth World Series was about to begin—the underdog Reds from the Queen City against the high and mighty White Sox from the Windy City.

The high and mighty of baseball were on hand for the annual gathering of the clans. The new owners of the Yankees, Colonel T.L. Huston and Colonel Jake Ruppert, were there; Harry Frazee, Broadway producer and owner of the Red Sox; Branch Rickey, who dreamed big dreams for St. Louis; Yankee manager Miller Huggins; Wilbert Robinson; John J. McGraw; Connie Mack; Clark Griffith; and Detroit manager Hughie Jennings. Tris Speaker, manager of the Indians, headed a Cleveland delegation of more than 500. And George M. Cohan of "Give My Regards to Broadway" fame was on hand, a passionate rooter. Many of the most prominent political figures of the Midwest and South were there, among them half a dozen governors, including James M. Cox of Ohio, honored guest for that first game.

The Reds were dressed in white home uniforms with red trim and piping. Their left sleeve fronts displayed a horseshoe "C" that curled around the words "Reds." Stirrup-type outer red stockings accentuated the team's image. Chicago players were clad in gray pin-striped road uniforms; their stockings were solid white. The left side of their uniform shirt sported a large blue "S." An "O" was inside the top curve of the "S" while an "X" was printed inside the lower curve.

The scheduled pitching matchup was Chicago's Eddie Cicotte against Cincinnati's Walter "Dutch" Ruether, 1919 National League leader in winning percentage with a 19–6 record.

DUTCH RUETHER: "All our players paid strict attention to Joe Jackson in batting practice. Up to that time no batter had ever hit a ball on the fly into the right-field bleachers. Joe poled three halfway into the bleachers."

Every seat in Redland Field was taken, and the overflow crowd congregated behind the temporary stands in front of the bleachers in right and left field. The game was played before 30,511 fans. All across America before radio broadcasts of this and every game of the Series would be followed by crowds of people who stood around for hours near newspaper shops and other stores observing the progress of the action through the movement of little figures on green boards. As far away as Cuba and Canada, each pitch, each ball, each strike, each swing, each run, hit, and error would be re-created by Western Union for waiting millions who paid for the privilege of listening to the recreation in halls and candy stores, in poolrooms and movie theaters.

Baseball writers of the time, covering those games played on grassy fields through languid days, had until three the next morning to file their stories for afternoon editions, plenty of time for full narratives and embellishments.

Up in the press box a who's who of the journalistic fraternity readied themselves: Taylor Spink of *The Sporting News,* Damon Runyon, Ring Lardner, a young Westbrook Pegler, Fred Lieb, and Hugh Fullerton in rimless glasses. Dubbed the game's greatest dopester, Fullerton's track record proved again and again that he was indeed the most accurate forecaster of his day. He had unhesitatingly predicted that the White Sox would easily win the Series.

Seated alongside Fullerton was the great Christy Mathewson, who had thrown his first major league pitch for the New York Giants on the afternoon of July 18, 1900, and had astonished the baseball world in 1905 with three World Series shutouts against Philadelphia. The image of "Matty" in the ragtime years leading the Giants out onto the field from the center field clubhouse at the Polo Grounds had been a familiar one to fans. At the end of the 1918 season Mathewson had enlisted in the Army. In Europe, the pitching immortal had been exposed to mustard gas at Flanders Field. Now returned from the war, Mathewson was at the Series as a correspondent for the Pulitzer chain of newspapers. Throughout the series he would sit close by Fullerton, circling in red questionable plays on a wirebound scorebook about the size of a sketchpad.

The anticipation level picked up in Redland Field as netted ropes were dragged across the diamond by turf levelers. Then the man known as the "March King," John Philip Sousa, stepped up on the band podium and began conducting the National Anthem. Fans, players, and the large press corps snapped to attention.

Game One

The White Sox did not score in the top of the first inning. The Reds came to bat against Eddie Cicotte, still ruffled a bit by an incident he had just experienced: on his way to the park a man on the street had told him that someone was looking for him with a rifle.

Cincinnati's leadoff batter was second baseman Maurice Rath, the same journeyman infielder who was sent along with Jackson in 1910 by Philadelphia to Cleveland for Brisco Lord. Cicotte's first pitch was a letter-high fastball. Rath took it for a strike. The next pitch hit Rath right between the shoulder blades. The plunking of Rath by Cicotte would later be reported as the signal that the Series was fixed. Jake Daubert singled Rath over to third base. Heinie Groh came to the plate with his distinctive bottle-shaped bat, fashioned to allow him to slide his hands upward to bunt or execute the hit and run. Close pitches twice sent Groh bailing out to the dirt. On the next pitch he gripped the bat a little firmer and made contact, slugging the ball to deep left field. Jackson caught up with it, but Rath tagged up and scored.

The game moved to the bottom of the fourth. The score was tied, 1–1. Pitching out of his big windup, Cicotte seemed to have things under control. With two outs and Larry Kopf the runner at second base, it seemed Cicotte might get through the inning. But Greasy Neale singled. Then Ivy Wingo singled. Kopf scored. Dutch Ruether, a notoriously weak-hitting pitcher, came to the plate. He gave a half smile to his teammates leading off second and third. Cicotte's first pitch to Ruether was a ball, low and off the plate. Ruether jumped on the next pitch. The ball headed to the fence in left center field. Neither Jackson nor Felsch could catch up with it. As they chased it down, the roar of the crowd seemed to triple in volume. Neale scored. Wingo scored. Ruether huffed and puffed his way into third base. Three runs for the Reds, and the inning wasn't over yet.

Gleason started up rookie right-hander Roy Wilkinson in the Chicago bullpen. Cicotte fidgeted around on the mound getting set to pitch to Rath. With the count 2–0, Rath ripped the ball past Weaver and down the line for a double. Then Jake Daubert shot the ball through the infield to right field for a single. Five straight hits. Five runs. An infuriated Kid Gleason would not even go out to the mound. He just stood on the baseline. "Cicotte," he screamed, "You're finished!" Wilkinson came in and retired Heinie Groh on a fly ball to center, and the inning was finally finished.

Jackson batted fourth in the Chicago lineup behind Buck Weaver and went 0 for 4. His final at bat of the game in the ninth inning came with the Sox losing, 9–1. He flew out to deep right field.

Greasy Neale, the only man to ever play in a World Series, coach a Rose Bowl football team, and be admitted to the Pro Football Hall of Fame as a coach, ripped out three hits for the Reds in the Series opener. Neale's good hitting never abated; he would bat .357 to lead all Cincinnati hitters in the series. Game One was also a showcase for Cincinnati pitcher Dutch Ruether, who held Chicago to six hits while pounding out two triples.

In the hotel lobbies around the American League, the White Sox of Chicago were often an elegant blur of diamond rings, pearl stickpins, silk shirts, and white cuffs adorned with elegant cufflinks extending two inches out from their expensive suit sleeves. But in the locker room after losing the first game of the World Series, they were anything but elegant. Eddie Cicotte was somber and silent along with the other White Sox. Only catcher Ray Schalk was animated, wondering out loud why Cicotte kept crossing him up on his signals.

Hugh Fullerton went around telling people, "I don't like what I saw out there today. There is something smelly. Cicotte doesn't usually pitch like that."

Cincinnati owner Garry Herrmann was elated over what he

had seen. Filled with pride after the game, he presided over a lavish party at the exclusive Peruvian Club. Each guest was presented with a barrel of pickels to be taken home as a gift.

The page-one story the next day in *The New York Times* read:

> The fondest dreams of Cincinnati's overjoyed baseball fans came true this afternoon when the Reds put the White Sox to rout. . . . Never before in the history of America's biggest baseball spectacle has a pennant-winning club received such a disastrous drubbing in an opening game as the far-famed White Sox got this afternoon. . . . The heralded White Sox looked like bush leaguers.

The banner headline in *The Chicago Daily Tribune* on Thursday, October 2, read WHITE SOX LOSE IN OPENER, 9–1. Three front-page stories headlined: ALL CINCINNATI HAILS RUETHER, MORAN'S BIG GUNS WHO CRIPPLED CICOTTE, ACE OF THE SOX HURLING CORPS, and REDS DRIVE CICOTTE TO DUGOUT; RUETHER HOLDS FOE HELPLESS."

The White Sox had problems; however, the multitude that attended the Series had problems of its own. Cincinnati was a city where no hotel rooms could be had. Thousands were put up in private homes, with some even sleeping in Turkish baths.

A *New York Times* article reported:

> The great crowds surged through the lobbies, and into the public parlors. Head waiters at the various hotel cafes were at their wits' ends when 9 o'clock arrived and the last of the diners had departed. Never were they faced with such a serious problem. . . . Hundreds of guests swarmed into the hotel dining rooms and demanded service. With every table filled and hundreds clamoring for entrance to the cafes, the head waiters' dilemma was complete. But the crowd was in a holiday mood and joked about the delay, despite the fact that everyone was hungry, after early luncheons.

Westbrook Pegler was one of the members of the press corps providing extensive coverage of the Series. He, along with the visiting White Sox and most of those covering the Series, was quartered at the Hotel Sinton, the best hotel in Cincinnati. Pegler reported that he "never saw as much loose money in a crap game. For three nights running they shot for hundred-dollar bills and they had sheaves of them."

With gamblers brazenly strutting their stuff, the rumors of a fixed Series were now intensifying. They reached Kid Gleason in the form of telegrams from concerned White Sox fans from several different states. Something crooked, the telegrams claimed, was going on in the World Series.

Gleason had been around baseball for a long time. He was fond of telling people that he had seen everything. Fixing a World Series, he thought, was an impossibility. The White Sox manager knew that too many players would have to cooperate for games to be dumped. But he was getting a bit suspicious.

Late that night after the first game, he met with Comiskey in his room in the Hotel Sinton, showed him the telegrams, and told his employer how he felt. Comiskey was noncommittal. He thanked Gleason for the information and said he would follow up. Then, though the hour was late, Comiskey went to John A. Heydler's room. Heydler in 1918 had succeeded John K. Tener as National League President. Comiskey told Heydler what Gleason had said.

JOHN A. HEYDLER: "You're wrought up too much, Commy. You're just being a bum loser. Your team was too confident and the Reds rushed them off their feet. They were taken unawares. You can't fix a World Series."

Some might have called Comiskey's heart-to-heart chat with Heydler "sleeping with the enemy," inasmuch as he was the president of the other league. But Comiskey had no alternative. He had not been on speaking terms with American League president Byron Bancroft "Ban" Johnson since 1917.

JOE JACKSON: "Mr. Comiskey had caught two big trout and they were such beauties he sent them to Mr. Johnson. He packed the fish in ice and expressed them, but by the time the fish got to Chicago the ice had melted and the fish had spoiled. They smelled awful."

Johnson always thought that Comiskey had insulted him, and that was why the two never spoke again and why the Chicago owner approached Heydler.

But now the two of them were outside Johnson's suite. It was about three A.M. The rooms and lobbies of the Hotel Sinton and Congress Hotel in Chicago that night and throughout the series resembled Hamlet's Elsinore Castle. There was much excitement and intrigue, secret meetings, loose women, and even looser men.

Upset and ruffled after being awakened by the knocking on his door, the heavyset Johnson was taken aback by the sight of Heydler and Comiskey on his doorstep. When Heydler explained their mission, an irritated Johnson snapped, "What he [Comiskey] says is like the crying of a whipped cur." And he closed the door.

Game Two
There were 29,698 in the stands on October 2, another warm day of what was being called the "first vestless series." The Reds were now favored by oddsmakers at 7–10. Lefty Williams was matched up for the White Sox against Cincinnati's thirty-five-year-old Harry "Slim" Sallee. It was the same Sallee who had lost two games to the White Sox in the 1917 World Series when he was a member of the New York Giants. "Watch Williams closely," Kid Gleason told Ray Schalk. The little catcher watched.

Black Betsy was smoking for Jackson in the second game. He led off the second inning and lined a double to center field, the first of his three hits in the game. Sacrificed to third by Felsch, he was stranded there as Gandil grounded out to short and Risberg flew out to right field.

Schalk kept watching Williams, who breezed through three innings. Then in the bottom of the fourth inning he walked Rath. Daubert sacrificed him to second. Groh walked. The noise level at Redland Field was picking up. Edd Roush singled to center, scoring Rath. Then Roush took off for second base. All the pent-up frustration in Schalk went into a powerful throw that gunned down the Cincinnati center fielder. Then Williams walked Duncan, his third free pass of the inning. Die-hard Chicago fans could never remember seeing the southpaw that wild. Williams had walked just 58 batters in 297 innings during the regular season. Larry Kopf, the Cincinnati shortstop and the sixth man in the batting order, came up to hit. He smashed a two-run triple. That was all the hitting and scoring the Reds needed. They won the game 4–2.

In the locker room, sweaty and disgusted, Schalk's fury was up a few notches after Chicago's second straight loss. "Three fucking times, three times," he told Kid Gleason, "Williams shook off my signals for curve balls."

Gleason tried to placate Schalk. It was baseball, he said, things like that could happen. But the little catcher would not agree. Then Gleason noticed a smug Gandil sitting around smiling.

"You sure had a good day today," Gleason snapped sarcastically.

"So did you, Kid!" was Gandil's wisecrack reply.

The comment so enraged Gleason that he rushed Gandil. It took the efforts of two players to pry his hands loose from Gandil's throat.

A shower and a change of clothes did not do much to soothe Ray Schalk's seething anger. His juices were flowing as he waited for Williams under the grandstand. When Williams came out, Schalk jumped the pitcher and pummeled him repeatedly with both fists until he, like Gleason, was pulled away by a couple of the other players.

Despite all the talk that was being bandied about of fixed games, there were still many who were not surprised that Cincinnati had won the first two games. Ruether and Sallee had won forty games between them during the regular season.

The Series shifted to Chicago for the third, fourth, and fifth games. A contingent of New York City sportswriters plus Col. T.L. Huston, half-owner of the Yankees, and John Orr, a stockholder in the Reds, were quartered in a private railroad car all during the Series. Their talk centered on the home-field advantage, the differences between the two leagues, and how gamblers played around with odds for their own special reasons.

One who shied away from most of that talk was thirty-four-year-old sportswriter Ring Lardner, a Chicagoan. He was also a fan of the White Sox. Two of his favorites on the team were Eddie Cicotte and Joe Jackson. Through the years Lardner had spent a lot of time on the road reading Katie Jackson's letters to her husband. He had also enjoyed drinking away the hours with Cicotte. After Game One was concluded, Lardner had a private chat with Cicotte and asked whether there was any truth to all the rumors going around.

"Bullshit," Cicotte said. "That's all it is."

Saying it was "bullshit," Lardner knew, did not make it so. Although he never put his fears into writing, Lardner was uncomfortable and agitated about the atmosphere that surrounded Cicotte, Jackson, the other White Sox players, and the Series. In the railroad car of the sleeper that carried players and press to Chicago for Game Three, he had more than his fill of alcohol. And then he lurched about singing, humming and, whistling a parody of "I'm Forever Blowing Bubbles":

> *I'm forever throwing ball games,*
> *Pretty ball games in the air.*
> *I come from Chi*
> *I hardly try*
> *Just to go to bat and fade and die:*
> *Fortune's coming my way:*
> *That's why I don't care.*
> *I'm forever blowing ball games,*
> *And the gamblers treat us fair.*

Once again Joseph Jefferson Jackson was part and apart from the scene as the White Sox and Reds, the press contingent, fans, gamblers, and assorted hangers-on made the all-night trek from Cincinnati to Chicago. For Joe Jackson the clickety-clack of train wheels, the hooting whistles in the night, the taste of whiskey and Pullman food, the smell of cigarette and cigar smoke, the sound of dirty jokes, laughter, confessions, the feel of rumpled clothes, the packing and unpacking and packing again—this had all long ago become ritual. Joe Jackson was a much different person after a decade in the majors with three different teams than when he made that first train ride up north to Philadelphia from Greenville. He had already played in one World Series, but this one was far different. The 1917 competition was between two major cities. This one was, he thought, the small guy, Cincinnati, against the giant, Chicago. The White Sox fans adored and loved their team, knew their baseball, were used to winning teams. From what he had seen of the Cincinnati fans, baseball to them was merely a carnival.

Special trains transported rabid Cincinnati rooters into Chicago. They turned it into their own personal parade grounds, singing and shouting all over the length and breadth of Michigan Boulevard. Thousands camped out all night, waiting outside festively decorated Comiskey Park to buy bleacher seats. By midmorning there were more than five thousand there.

And vivid red was everywhere—red dresses, shirts, flags, pennants, banners. The vast Congress Hotel in Chicago was swept up in a sea of red. Reds fans by the thousands were there, and ready.

Game Three
On October 3, rookie southpaw "Wee Dickie" Kerr took the mound for the White Sox in Comiskey Park before 29,126, most of whom were there to cheer on the team in white. They were ready with streamers of blue and white, noisemakers to accentuate the moment, and sweaters and coats to stave off the cutting edge of the chill that blew in off the lake.

Joe Jackson led off the second inning singling to left field. A hurried throw to second by Reds pitcher Ray Fisher on Felsch's bunt went into the outfield. Jackson took third; Felsch wound up on second base. Then Gandil slapped the ball up the middle through the drawn-in infield for a single and two RBIs.

That was all the scoring the White Sox needed. Kerr, constantly encouraged by the shouts of his infielders, was a master on the mound, allowing only three Reds to get as far as second base. He hurled a three-hit shutout as the White Sox won, 3–0, in a game that took just ninety minutes to play. Adolfo Luque hurled one inning in relief for the Reds, becoming the first Latin American player to appear in a World Series.

Afterwards, *The New York Times* had this to say about Kerr's glittering moment:

> Not so long ago Dicky Kerr was a professional boxer out in Milwaukee. He was a bantam and could take a beating and give one. Instead of a wild lefthander shaking with stage fright in the face of the Redland troupe, Kerr looked them over with nerves of chilled steel.

There were those on the inside who also noted that the offensive power that won for Kerr and the White Sox was supplied by Jackson, Risberg, Gandil, and Felsch—all members of the faction on the team that the little Texan did not belong to. They were those who also noted how Jackson's stroke had come alive. His two singles in three at bats in that third game gave him five hits in his last seven at bats. He was batting .435 for the series.

Game Four

Cicotte was slated to pitch the fourth game against Cincinnati's Jimmy Ring. Kid Gleason had his doubts. But "Chubby Eddie Cicotte," *The New York Times* reported, ". . . begged manager Kid Gleason to let him go in. Eddie wanted to vindicate himself for his failure in the opening clash in Redland."

Game-time temperature was about 70 degrees, and Cicotte seemed to thrive in it. His pitching was back on track. But his fielding was atrocious.

What many saw as a pivotal play or non-play in the game took place in the fifth inning. Cicotte awkwardly attempted to field an infield tapper by Pat Duncan but wound up throwing the ball into the outfield. Duncan made it all the way to second base. Larry Kopf hit the ball into left field, and Jackson uncorked one of his patented throws to the plate in an attempt to cut down Duncan. But Cicotte waved at Jackson's throw to the plate. It seemed he was trying to stop the ball. He only managed to deflect it, and Duncan scored easily. To most observers it was obvious that Jackson's throw would have nailed Duncan had it not been cut off. A double by Neale then scored Kopf.

The twenty-four-year-old Jimmy Ring, who had his curve ball snapping, pitched one of the best games of his career. He allowed just three hits, by Jackson, Gandil, and Felsch. The Reds won, 2–0. Cicotte had made just three errors during the regular season, but his two fielding errors in the fifth inning allowed the only two runs to score. And the talk again started up about the White Sox. A team that had always found ways to win was now finding ways to lose.

That night Chicago's Loop was a swarm of red. Cincinnati fans, boosted by the ragtime strains of a band, drank and sang and stumbled their way through the streets. Some of them were still there as morning dawned.

Sunday, October 5, was the date for the scheduled fifth game of the World Series. But there would be no game that day. After four consecutive Indian summer sunny days, rain fell. It became a day for the White Sox to lick their wounds, and for the Reds to collect their thoughts. The Chicago players sat in their clubhouse at Comiskey Park fingering gloves and picking imaginary splinters out of their bats. There was an edginess and a silence that was broken from time to time with recriminations. Several players taunted each other about pitches that should have been better, throws that could have been more accurate, balls that could have been fielded more crisply.

Kid Gleason was doing most of the talking to the raft of reporters hovering about him. Luck, he told them, was something that could swing from team to team, and up to now the White Sox had been out of luck. He made the point that he still believed his team was the best one to ever go into a World Series. Sure, he said, his club was down three games to one, but he still was certain that his crowd would come back.

Joe Jackson half-listened to all the talking; he had very little to say. Working on his glove with a little bit of sweet oil, stretching out his long legs before his locker, and chewing tobacco, he kept himself busy. His dark eyes avoided contact with anyone. In his mind he was playing at the top of his game—flawless in the field, hitting better than anyone on the White Sox. He did not like the atmosphere in the clubhouse.

Game Five

Although Gleason had said he would not use Lefty Williams when his pitching turn came up again—"I think I'll go in myself," he'd said—Williams took the mound for the White Sox against Hod Eller, a specialist in trick deliveries.

Umpire Cy Rigler, a hulk of a man who had started the tradition in the minors in 1905 of umpires raising their right hand to signify strikes, watched the battle play out from behind home plate. Williams was in all-star form; Eller was in Hall of Fame form. In the second and third innings, the Indiana native struck out six White Sox in a row: Gandil, Risberg, Schalk, then Williams, Leibold, and Collins. In the fourth inning Eller retired Weaver and Jackson on infield grounders and struck out Felsch. Williams did not give up a hit until Kopf singled with two outs in the fifth inning.

Through five innings the game played out—a double shutout. This was the kind of baseball the 34,379 fans had come to see, tight, taut, and heads-up all the way.

But in the sixth inning it all came apart for Williams. Eller doubled to left center, the ball falling in between Jackson and Felsch. The moment was described in *Reach's 1920 Official Guide:* "Jackson seemed to be day-dreaming when Eller's fly was hit in his direction." Then a single by Rath to right scored Eller. Daubert laid down a sacrifice bunt to Weaver. Rath took third. Heinie Groh worked the count full. The he walked on what many thought was a questionable call. Schalk was in a fury and screamed and spit at Rigler, who avoided confrontation. Edd Roush was next. He caught a pitch on the fat part of his bat for a booming blast to deep center, Happy Felsch's territory. The White Sox center fielder raced for the ball, seemed to lose it for a moment, and caught up with it. Then a two-handed lunge and the ball was in his glove for an instant. It fell out, and Felsch was all arms and legs scurrying about to pick it up. Rath scored. Groh headed for home, and there were those who swore later they heard Edd Roush screaming, "Get running, you crooked son of a bitch." Felsch cut loose a powerful throw to Eddie Collins, who relayed the ball to Schalk. The ball and Groh seemed to arrive at the same time. Schalk put the tag on, but Rigler screamed "Safe! Safe!" Livid, Schalk cursed and bumped the umpire. He was thrown out of the game and replaced by second-string catcher Bird Lynn.

That was the least of it. The Reds wound up with a four-run sixth inning. They won the game, 5–0. Eller hurled a three-hitter and struck out nine. An interesting postscript to Eller's performance was that before the series started he had told Cincinnati manager Moran that he had turned down a $5,000 bribe from gamblers. Moran permitted Eller to pitch but told him, "I'm gonna watch your every twitch out on the field."

Every twitch of the White Sox players was watched out on the field by Kid Gleason. Through the five games his offense had failed to score a run in 41 of the 45 innings played. They had been shut out in their last 22 innings. They had scored but six runs in the entire five games. He knew it was a batting slump, a terrible batting slump. Joe Jackson, he thought, was caught knee-deep in it, not even getting the ball out of the infield in that fifth game: three popups and a ground out.

Newspapers announced after the fifth game that the players' World Series shares would be $5,000 each for the winners and $3,254 for the losers. Baseball's National Commission would pocket the proceeds for the remaining games.

Game Six

On October 7, Game Six was about to get under way in Cincinnati, a city burning with World Series fever. More than 32,000 were in the stands at Redland Field. More than 10,000 had been turned away. With Chicago down four games to one, most conceded victory in the Series to the Reds. After four innings, with the home team leading 4–0, it certainly looked that way. The White Sox had now gone twenty-six innings without scoring. Then they suddenly woke up, scoring a run in the top of the fifth—their first run since Game Three. In the sixth, after a Weaver double, an RBI single to center by Jackson, a double by Felsch that scored Jackson, and a single by Schalk that scored Felsch, the score was tied.

The game and starter Dickie Kerr labored on into extra innings. In the top of the tenth, Weaver doubled, and advanced to second on a bunt beat out by Jackson. Gandil singled in Weaver, and the White Sox had a 5–4 triumph.

Joe Jackson, not one to suffer mood swings or show that much emotion, admitted later, "I got a mighty big kick out of the two games Dickie Kerr pitched and won for us. That was something."

Like the boxer that he once was, Dickie Kerr was on the ropes throughout the game. He gave up eleven hits, but he stayed the distance. And like a prizefighter coming off the ropes, the White Sox seemed to have awakened. Their bats, Kid Gleason thought, were popping at last. The batting slump was over. They could still pull this thing off.

Game Seven

On October 8 only 13,923 fans showed up, less than half the capacity of the Redland ballpark. The thinking was the fans were disappointed at Cincinnati's defeat in Game Six. The mood around the White Sox and their supporters was up; the four hits pounded out in the sixth inning the day before showed what Chicago was capable of doing. Today, with Cicotte on the mound, the talk in the dugout was that there was hope for another win. Gleason was going around telling everyone that his top pitcher would prevail.

As if they believed this, the Reds were especially vituperative, some would say vulgar, in the pregame bench jockeying.

They tried their best to distract Cicotte as he threw his warmup pitches. But he would have no part of such distraction. Honed in, looking at Schalk's glove and home plate, throwing the ball—that was Cicotte's entire world.

It carried over through the game. After five innings the White Sox led 4–0. Cicotte was a master, spacing seven hits and throttling the Reds, 4–1. Joe Jackson's first-inning single to left scored Shano Collins. His two-out single to left in the third inning again drove in Collins.

It seemed that the Sox were finally back on track.

Game Eight
On October 9, the teams took the field at Comiskey park for the eighth game. There were 32,930 in the stands, pushing the total Series attendance to 236,928, a record for that period. Many of the fans believed the White Sox, trailing four games to three, would win and deadlock the series. But a gambler, as the story goes, told Hugh Fullerton, "All the betting's on Cincinnati! It's going to be the biggest first inning you ever saw."

The game matched up Lefty Williams in his third start for the Sox against Hod Eller of Cincinnati. Williams, who would later say he received a death threat on the telephone the night before the game, walked Rath, the Reds leadoff batter. Then Daubert, Groh, and Roush singled. Duncan doubled. After throwing just fourteen pitches, Williams was finished. So were the White Sox. The Cincinnati lead stretched to 10–1 by the eighth inning, when Chicago scored four runs. It was too little and much too late. The final out of the 1919 World Series was made by Joe Jackson when he grounded out to second baseman Maurice Rath with two men on.

The Reds were World Champions.

The White Sox were in disgrace.

In that eighth game Joe Jackson had a two-for-five day, came in all the way from first base on a single, hit the only homer in the Series, and drove in three runs to cap off a .375 batting average and a .563 slugging percentage. His batting average in the 1919 Series led all hitters and was 71 points higher than what he had managed in 1917. He played flawlessly in the field throughout the series, handling thirty balls in the outfield; he made no errors. His twelve hits were a new World Series record. It was originally thirteen. But a hot grounder that Rath at second was unable to make a play on was changed to an error for Rath rather than a hit for Jackson.

By any stretch of the imagination it would have seemed that the 1919 World Series performance of Joe Jackson was indeed that of a player beyond reproach.

On the other hand, Eddie Collins batted just .226 with two errors while Nemo Leibold hit .056 in eighteen at bats. Roush, the National League batting champ, hit but .214, and his fellow batting star Heinie Groh finished with a .172 average.

That night, after the final game of the World Series, Lefty Williams came into Jackson's suite at the Lexington Hotel. He had been drinking, and he held two dirty envelopes in his hand. "One of these is for you, Joe. Some of us players sold the Series to a gambling clique. We told the clique that you would play crooked ball, too. There's $5,000 in the envelope. It's not all what we were promised, but it's better than getting nothin'."

JOE JACKSON: "I told Williams I didn't want the money and that he had a hell of a lot of nerve using my name in the affair. Also I told him that I was going to tell Comiskey just what had happened."

Williams, reeling about the room, threw the envelope down on the floor and left. Katie was in the bathroom, and when she came out, Joe told her what had happened. "What an awful thing to do," she said.

The following day with $5,000 in his pocket, Joe Jackson went to see Comiskey at his office in the ballpark. In a kind of symbolic show of arrogance and power, Comiskey always kept the door to his office locked. Anyone seeking entrance had to knock on the drawn wooden shutters. Jackson knocked. Harry Grabiner, the quasi-general manager and secretary to Comiskey came to the door. "The old man isn't feeling well," Grabiner said. "Go home, Joe. We know what you want."

Jackson and his black bats. When he went back home to winter in South Carolina, he took his beloved bats along: "Bats don't like to freeze no more than me." *(Chicago Historical Society)*

Knuckleballer Eddie Cicotte possessed pinpoint control and an expert ability to change speeds. *(Library of Congress)*

Center fielder Happy Felsch owned nearly as much range as the great Tris Speaker and had a powerful throwing arm. *(National Baseball Library)*

Buck Weaver was the only third baseman Ty Cobb would not bunt against. *(NBL)*

Second baseman Eddie Collins: "The smartest man that ever walked on a ball field." *(NBL)*

Shortstop Swede Risberg had a flashy style, a powerful arm, and a quick temper. In the minors he had once kayoed an umpire with just one punch after a dispute over a called third strike. *(NBL)*

Lefty Williams was a master of the sweeping curve, and he had a lofty .652 winning percentage in his four full major league seasons. *(NBL)*

Chick Gandil was a steady hitter and a slick first baseman. *(NBL)*

Utility infielder Fred McMullin was a valuable reserve. *(NBL)*

Ty Cobb and Jackson. The "Georgia Peach" and the "Caroline Confection" were constantly compared. The fellow southerners shared the American League spotlight for a decade. *(NBL)*

ager Kid Gleason: "A rough, tough
w who would fight his weight in
cats." *(NBL)*

White Sox owner Charles Comiskey and
Cubs president Bill Veeck at the 1923 Cook
County Grand Jury hearings. *(NBL)*

ge Kenesaw Mountain Landis: "He typified the heights to which dramatic talent may carry a
in America if only he has the foresight not to go on stage." *(NBL)*

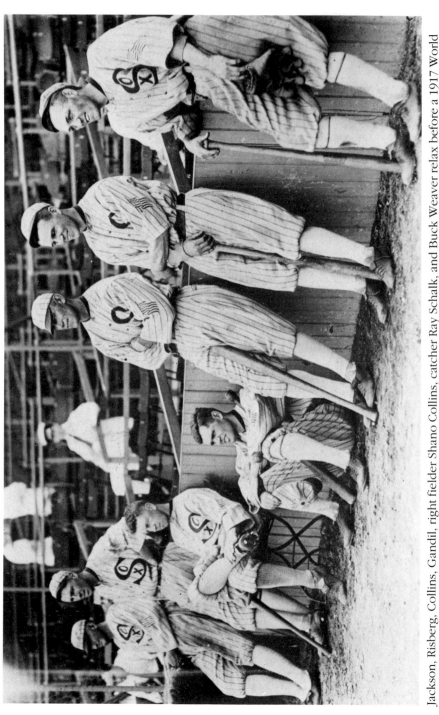

Jackson, Risberg, Collins, Gandil, right fielder Shano Collins, catcher Ray Schalk, and Buck Weaver relax before a 1917 World Series game. *(CHS)*

During the 1917 season, major league teams held close order drill for an hour each day; even the mighty White Sox, shown here, went through their paces before a game. Weaver and Felsch are on the left and Jackson is third from the right.   (CHS)

The second game of the 1919 World Series: Chick Gandil is called out attempting to steal second base. *(CHS)*

The Black Sox in court with their attorneys: (seated from left) attorney William Fallon, Jackson, Weaver, Cicotte, Risberg, Williams, Gandil. (Felsch must have stepped out, and the case against McMullin had been dropped due to insufficient evidence.) *(CHS)*

Jackson played with mill teams, outlaw barnstormers, and the semipros for almost twenty more years. Although he often changed his name to avoid detection, his unmistakable swi... always gave him away. *(NBL)*

But Jackson persisted, displaying the $5,000 to Grabiner, telling him how he had come by it, asking him what to do about it.

JOE JACKSON: "Grabiner told me to take the money and go to my home in Savannah. He told me if anything further was to be done, he or Comiskey would write me about it. Then he slammed the door on me."

The day after the Series ended, Hugh Fullerton wrote in his column:

> There will be a great deal written about the World Series. There will be a lot of inside stuff that never will be printed. The truth will remain that the team which was the hardest working . . . won. The team . . . which had the individual ability was beaten. They spilled the dope terribly. . . . So much so that an evil-minded person might believe the stories that have been circulated during the Series. The fact is, this Series was lost in the first game.
>
> Yesterday's, in all probability, is the last game that will ever be played in any World Series. If the club owners and those who have the interest of the game at heart, have listened during the Series, they will call off the annual inter-league contest . . . . Yesterday's game also means the disruption of the Chicago White Sox ball club. There are seven men on the team who will not be there when the gong sounds next spring.

The Fullerton articles appeared and were scoffed at as muckraking sensationalism. In actuality, that's all they were. Fullerton violated all the rules of journalism. He later admitted that he based what he wrote solely on unconfirmed and unchecked rumors.

CHARLES COMISKEY: "There is always some scandal of some kind following a big sporting event like the World Series. These yarns are manufactured out of whole cloth and grow out of bitterness due to losing wagers. I believe my boys fought the battles of the recent World Series on the level, as they have always done, and I would be the first to want information to the contrary."

All denials to the contrary, with the Series over charges of a fix were now out in the open. Controversy erupted. Strong statements poured forth from all quarters. Charge and counter-charge ensued. Rumor and denial intermingled.

The Sporting News in 1919 advertised Camel cigarettes for 19 cents a pack. A Wrigley's gum ad said "a little stick of Wrigley's makes the whole world kin." A.J. Reach ad copy for its punching bags read: "Bag punching is an interesting and healthful exercise—striking bags bearing the Reach Trade Mark are perfect shape and swing true." But *Sporting News* readers were far less interested in the ads than they were in the comments of correspondent Joe Vila, whose story on the series carried headlines like: REDS WON FAIR AND SQUARE AND DESERVE ALL HONORS and WHITE SOX SHOULD NOT HAVE BEEN ALLOWED TO EASE UP AND BURLESQUE IN THE FINAL GAMES OF SEASON.

WESTBROOK PEGLER: "I was one of the reporters throughout the Series. In the lobby of the Sinton hotel, George M. Cohan, Mr. Broadway himself, said something which should have brought my ears up. I asked him to do a song about the Series for the United News Wire. He had written 'Over There' in forty-five minutes. This Series was trivial by comparison with the World War, so I thought he ought to be able to knock one out in fifteen minutes. Cohan laughed and said the Series was beneath his artistic notice. After all that war had not been a frame-up."

College-educated William "Billy" Evans, who in 1906 at age twenty-two had become the youngest umpire in history, had plied his trade in the 1919 series. "Well, I guess I'm just a big dope," he said afterwards. "That Series looked all right to me."

ROGER PECKINPAUGH: "I played against them many times and knew the team well, watching them from my shortstop po-sition with the Yankees. You just never knew when they were going to go out there and beat your brains out or roll over and play dead. Somebody was betting on those games, that's a cinch. When they wanted to play, you had a hard time beating them, that's how good they were."

One of those who attended the World Series was Ray Chapman, who had been Jackson's teammate on Cleveland five years before. When he returned home after the Series, Chapman was asked if he had done any betting. He said he'd wagered nothing since "something didn't feel right."

John Foster, the editor of the *Spalding Guide,* claimed that the alleged baseball experts did not have enough appreciation for the teamwork of the Reds, the pitching of Ruether, Sallee, and Ring, and the fine hitting of Edd Roush.

The jubilant Cincinnati Reds, their pride stung by the charges of a fix, went on the offensive, defending their legitimate claim to the world championship. Cincinnati manager Pat Moran, given a $5,000 bonus for his accomplishments, was especially annoyed at all the talk of "dumped games."

PAT MORAN: "Even if the White Sox did throw games, we were the better team and would have won with the games played on the level. If they threw some of the games, they must be consummate actors, and their place is on the stage, for nothing in their playing gave us the impression they weren't doing their best. While the Reds were never worried about the outcome, they had to go the limit to win. And it is an astonishing thing to me that Cicotte, Risberg, Weaver, Jackson, and Felsch could get away with that sort of thing and us never know it."

JIMMY RING: "They played like horseshit, but we would have beaten them anyway."

HEINIE GROH: "Cicotte put everything on the ball when pitching to me, and I found his delivery as hard to solve as any I had faced all year. Our suspicions were never aroused as they seemed to be doing their level best to win. We attributed the stories heard around Cincinnati about the White Sox not trying to 'sour grapes' on the part of the American League sympathizers. As to Risberg, he robbed one of our fellows of a triple and saved three runs when he leaped high in the air and speared a liner with bases full. If he missed that he could not have possibly been accused of lying down."

EDD ROUSH: "Why, I didn't get a bingle off Cicotte and every time I faced him he seemed to have a world of speed. I can't yet see how they could play the way they did and throw the games. It is a mystery to me."

Lost in all the headlines and recriminations was White Sox pitcher Urban Clarence Faber, who had missed the Series because of a sore ankle.

RAY SCHALK: "If Red had been able to pitch I'm sure there would have been no Black Sox scandal."

Hugh Fullerton wrote for the *Chicago Herald and Examiner,* but the newspaper refused to publish any amplification of his charges. The only newspaper in the country that picked up his story was Joseph Pulitzer's *New York Evening World*.

Charles Comiskey offered a $10,000 reward for any evidence that would prove his players intentionally sought to dump games. Then he met with Maclay Hoyne, state's attorney for Cook County, and told him that he believed he had been "jobbed." The "Old Roman" requested help and said he would take care of all the investigative expenses.

In an October 1919 editorial J.G. Taylor Spink, publisher of *The Sporting News,* attacked Fullerton and others whom he claimed had sullied the national pastime.

> Because a lot of dirty, long-nosed, thick-lipped and strong smelling gamblers butted into the World Series—an American event by the way—and some of said gentlemen got crossed, stories were peddled that there was something wrong with the way the games were played . . . Comiskey has met that by offering $10,000 for any sort of a clue that will bear out such a charge . . . There will be no takers because there is no such evidence, except in the mucky minds of the stinkers who—because they are crooked—think all the rest of the world can't play straight.

Spink's none-too-subtle anti-Semitic jab was at the "King of the Gamblers," Arnold Rothstein. His defense of the purity of the game notwithstanding, however, forces had been set loose that could not be stopped. A momentum had begun that would change baseball forever.

Four distinct investigations resulted from the Fullerton articles. Heydler, Comiskey, Bill Veeck of the Cubs, and Ban Johnson all hired detectives.

An editorial in the November 1919 issue of *Baseball Magazine* lambasted Fullerton: "If a man really knows so little about baseball that he believes the game is or can be fixed, he should keep his mouth shut when in the presence of intelligent people."

Undaunted, Hugh Fullerton persisted like a bulldog. Repetition and amplification of his charges were published in the *New York World* in December of 1919 while the owners conducted their winter meetings.

He also made it known that his own investigation had proved fruitless and related that "St. Louis parties" came to Chicago at his direction and all they were able to do was provide hearsay evidence. The only indiscretions reported by the detectives hired by Comiskey were the comments of Cicotte: "Don't worry about me. I got mine." This was supposedly said by the White Sox pitcher to a relative after the Series. And there was a telegram that Gandil was alleged to have sent to his wife before the series began: I HAVE BET MY SHOES. When the Series was over, Gandil spent money very freely. Some wondered where it came from.

Comiskey at first held back the $3,000 World Series checks earned by all the suspected players; pressure from the players and the advice of his attorneys finally convinced him to release the money. He renewed his offer of a $10,000 reward for information of a fix. "If I had the goods on any of my ballplayers," Comiskey said, "I will see that there is no place in organized ball for them."

7

1920

The 1920 census recorded the population of the United States at 106,466,000. In 1900, there were but 15 million newspapers sold in the United States. Now that circulation was more than 33 million. Although many people were caught up in the front-page stories about the Sacco and Vanzetti case, many more purchased newspapers to read about sports—especially baseball.

A Dallas newspaper covering the 1920 presidential election reported: "Ohio has two contenders for the presidency of the United States and one for the baseball championship of the world. Ask anyone in the state who is going to win and they'll answer 'Cleveland.' It would never occur to anyone to think that the questioner might be referring to Ohioan Cox or Harding and the trifling matter of the country's presidency."

The bestselling books of 1920 included F. Scott Fitzgerald's *This Side of Paradise,* Sinclair Lewis's *Main Street* and Sherwood Anderson's *Winesburg, Ohio.* Clara Bow and Rudolph Valentino were the idols of moviegoers. It was the time of Bill Tilden in tennis, Bobby Jones in golf, and Jack Dempsey in boxing. People all over the country were humming a brand-new song, "Whispering."

The appearance of the lively ball—or whatever it was that caused offensive production to jump so dramatically—and the sale of Babe Ruth to the New York Yankees were two events in 1920 that would change baseball history. On January 5, the

Yankees purchased Babe Ruth's contract from the Boston Red Sox. The purchase price was $100,000 (one-fourth of it cash) plus $25,000 a year at 6% interest. The extraordinary deal also included a $300,000 loan to the Red Sox with Fenway Park as collateral. It bailed out financially strapped Harry Frazee, the Red Sox owner. But what would be called "the curse of the Bambino" would forever alter the images of the New York Yankees and Boston Red Sox.

The lively baseball made its appearance when the A.J. Reach Company, manufacturer of the official American League ball, and Spalding, maker of the National League ball, switched to Australian yarn, which was stronger than American yarn. With balls wound tighter, they became harder and bouncier, triggering spiraling home run totals. With more new balls being used in games, and the new ban on the spitter, run production shot sky-high. Babe Ruth was one of the chief beneficiaries. He would hit a record 54 home runs that season of 1920. Perhaps he should have been credited with 55.

JOE JACKSON: "We were playing the Yankees a pretty important series in Chicago. The crowd was roped off on the field. Babe Ruth kissed one into the crowd and I jumped in after it. The umpire, Tommy Connolly, called Ruth out. I never touched the ball."

In January 1920, the National Commission, the ruling body of baseball, announced that it was expending every effort to stop gambling. There had been just too much negative publicity about the 1919 World Series. Ban Johnson let it be known that he had hired a detective agency to supervise private police in American League ballparks to ferret out evidence of gamblers.

When the 1919 World Series ended, Ray Schalk had issued some strong statements about crossups and fixes. As the new year of 1920 began, Schalk echoed what Fullerton had charged—that seven White Sox players would not return for the 1920 season. Then on January 16, responding to what was obviously pressure from Comiskey, Schalk reversed himself.

RAY SCHALK: "I played to the best of my ability. I feel that every man on our club did the same, and there was not a single moment of all the games in which we did all not try. How anyone can say differently if he saw the Series is a mystery to me."

On February 12, the Negro National Baseball League (National Association of Colored Professional Baseball Clubs) was formed in Kansas City, Missouri. Rube Foster, owner of the Chicago American Giants, created the new league. There were eight franchises located in midwestern cities, the first organized structure of black teams.

Black baseball of the ragtime era was a clouded mirror in which major league baseball could see its earlier self. Until Foster made his move black baseball lived under an ad-hoc organizational framework of pickup teams and sporadic schedules. In 1900, black stars earned $466 a year, a hundred dollars less than the average salary of white minor leaguers, and much less than the $2,000 average salary of white major leaguers. There are accounts of black players barred from hotels, wandering about the streets at night looking for a bench to sleep on.

The Chicago Leland Giants of 1907 were named for Frank C. Leland. The team's superstar was Rube Foster, whom Honus Wagner called "the smartest pitcher I have ever seen in all my years in baseball." The Kansas City Monarchs of 1908 were chiefly made up of former college athletes. The New York Lincoln Giants were managed by their star, John Henry "Pop" Lloyd, who was called the "Black Wagner." Said Wagner, "I am honored to have John Lloyd called the Black Wagner. It is a privilege to have been compared with him."

Just about the time the Negro National League was formed, Harry Grabiner took the train from Chicago to Savannah to visit Jackson. After the 1919 World Series, Comiskey had paid out bonuses of $3,000 each to Felsch and Cicotte and $875 to Williams. Then, although it is clear that he had full knowledge of who the accused players were, the Old Roman went about signing players for the 1920 season at much higher salaries than ever before. Cicotte's paycheck jumped from $5,000 to almost $10,000. Williams was signed for $6,000, doubling what he had earned in 1919. Happy Felsch saw his salary increased from $4,000 to $7,000. But Joe Jackson had returned his contract unsigned. Newspaper stories speculated that he was thinking of retiring from baseball and concentrating solely on his business interests if he were not able to come to terms with the White Sox.

Intent on signing Jackson, Comiskey dispatched Grabiner to Savannah. Grabiner called from the station, and Jackson picked him up. They drove around the city talking about baseball and other things. Then the dour Grabiner, annoyed with the newspaper stories about Jackson, got down to business.

"We've got the goods on Cicotte, Williams, and Gandil," said Grabiner. "We know who was guilty in throwing the Series. We know it all and how much each man got in being crooked. We know you discussed fixing the World Series with Gandil, and that Williams gave you $5,000."

The words infuriated Jackson. All that offseason he had smarted. The memory of his going to Comiskey's office prepared to tell all he knew about the fix and hand over the $5,000, only to have Grabiner slam the door in his face, still piqued him. Especially since he subsequently had received a letter from Comiskey advising him his presence might be needed in Chicago if an investigation was started.

JOE JACKSON: "I wrote Comiskey, or rather, my wife wrote in my name, that I would be glad to go there anytime. I never heard from Comiskey after that about the Series or the money."

But now Grabiner, who had his own agenda, was dismissing out of hand all the items on Jackson's agenda.

"We've made our own private investigation," he said. "But let's drop all this talk now and get down to the contract."

Jackson was perplexed. "Wait up, will you, Mr. Grabiner. I still have the money you told me to take. What am I to do about it? What should I do with it?"

"You can keep it as that's the only sensible thing. Or you give it to me. Cicotte, Williams, and the others have wrongfully used your name. But let's talk contract."

Jackson resisted: "My sister is ill and in the hospital. I don't much feel like talking about money right now."

"Let's get it done. I came all the way here to get it done. The offer is an iron-clad contract—no ten day reserve clause. Three years at $8,000 a year."

"I want $10,000 for the coming season. Only Ty Cobb had a better batting average than me last year. I'll probably do even better this year."

"You can take what I'm offering or you can leave it. You well know we can do what we want with you, with any of you. You take it or we kick you out of baseball."

"But I wanna have Katie look it over."

"There's no time for me to wait around for all of that. You sign and get it over with."

Sitting there in the car with Harry Grabiner pointing out where to sign, Joe Jackson painstakingly scrawled out his signature on a three-year contract. To him, signing his name was just copying a design Katie had taught him. He still did not know how to write.

And he still did not know how to read.

The contract contained these words: "The club holds in reserve the right to terminate for cause, all obligations as stipulated above, ten days immediately following its notification to the signee."

While Grabiner went South after Jackson, Comiskey headed out West to personally negotiate with Chick Gandil and Swede Risberg. Gandil asked for a $20,000 raise. Comiskey turned him down. He signed with a team in the Pacific Coast League and announced that he was opening a restaurant in San Francisco. Risberg and Comiskey could not come to contract terms, and the Swede decided to hold out.

That season of 1920 the White Sox began spring training in Waco, Texas. It was essentially the same team that had won the pennant the year before except for the missing Risberg and Gandil. Twenty-nine-year-old Buck Weaver, in his prime and knowing other teams were interested in his services, held out. It did not do him much good. Comiskey would not budge. Reluctantly, Weaver signed a contract for $7,000 and reported to spring training just a bit late.

Among the White Sox, all talk of the scandal in the 1919 World Series faded. Two days before the start of the season Risberg finally signed his contract. Comiskey was satisfied that his boys had the stuff to win it all in 1920.

For the new season major league club owners raised the price of bleacher seats to fifty cents, pavilion to seventy-five cents, and grandstand to a dollar. An option was granted to teams to set aside space in the bleachers at fifteen cents and twenty-five cents for children under fourteen years of age.

Although beer was banned in ballparks in 1920, Sunday games were played everywhere except Boston, Pittsburgh, and Philadelphia. In St. Louis, fans were excited by the hitting of two infielders: Rogers Hornsby of the Cardinals and George Sisler of the Browns. Both would win batting titles that season.

The joint rules committee of the major leagues banned the spitter in 1920 and declared illegal all foreign substances applied to baseballs: sandpaper, paraffin, cutting devices, hair oil.

SAM CRAWFORD: "Ed Walsh's spitter. . . . I think the ball disintegrated on the way to the plate, and the catcher put it together again. I swear when it went past the plate just the spit went by."

Seventeen pitchers were "grandfathered" as legalized spitballers for the remainder of their careers: Yancy "Doc" Ayers and Hubert "Dutch" Leonard of the Tigers, Ray Caldwell and Stan Coveleski of the Indians, Urban "Red" Faber of the White Sox, Jack Quinn of the Yankees, Allen Russell of the Red Sox, Urban Schocker and Allen Sothoron of the Browns, Bill Doak and Marv Goodwin of the Cardinals, Phil Douglas of the Giants, Dana Fillingim and Dick Rudolph of the Braves, and Burleigh Grimes and Clarence Mitchell of the Dodgers.

The White Sox moved out to a fast start, winning their first six games and dominating the league most of April. Joe Jackson was off fast too, flailing away as though consciously attempting to exorcise a demon, to remove all mention of the World Series fix.

A product of the Bronx, Al Schacht claimed he was born on the future site of Yankee Stadium. He would become known as "the Clown Prince of Baseball" because of his screwball entertaining antics. But in 1920 Schacht was just a young pitcher and new on the Washington club.

AL SCHACHT: "Joe Jackson was the best hitter on the greatest team I ever saw. . . . This is in 1920, before they have got on to the White Sox, and they are ripping and tearing up and down the league and they move into Washington. I am just a young fellow and new on the Washington club, but I am going very good . . . and Griff [Clark Griffith] says to me—Griff is managing the ball club then: 'You are going to pitch today. Now, there is one thing I want to tell you—and I want you to remember it: Don't throw a fastball to Jackson. Throw him your screwball. Throw him your screwball,' Griff says. 'If he hits it I can't kick. I don't care if he hits it over the fence. But whatever you do, don't throw him your fastball.'

"That was in the clubhouse. When we got out to the bench, I says to George McBride: 'What's going on here? Griff tells me not to throw a fastball to Jackson and that's all. What about Risberg and Collins and Felsch and the rest of those guys? Don't they count? Is Jackson the only hitter on the club?'

" 'No,' George says, 'Griff just has Jackson on his mind.'

"Well, the game starts and Risberg leads off, and I pitch him one ball, and he hits it to left field for a single. Felsch is next, and he hits the next pitch to right field for a single. I am doing great. Two pitches and there are men on first and second and up comes Collins . . . he pops up, which is a great break for me. At least I have got somebody out. I am feeling very happy but I do not feel very happy for long because the next hitter is Jackson.

"Gharrity, who is catching for us, signs for a fastball. I can't believe the sign, and I ask him to give it to me again, and he comes right back with it. Well, I am in a hell of a spot. Griff tells me not to pitch a fastball to Jackson, and here is Gharrity calling for it, and I am just a young fellow on the ball club and I can't shake off a fellow like Gharrity. Besides how do I know Griff hasn't changed his mind?

"I throw him a fastball inside with everything I can put on it, and he hits it to the right-field corner. Risberg and Felsch are tearing around the bases, and Jackson is rounding first base and I am on my way to back up at third base—and I almost run head on into Griff. He has come out of the dugout like he was shot out of it, and he is screaming at me: 'You're out of the ball game. You're out of the ball game.'

"I always claim that is a record. Jackson is just turning round second base on his way to third—and I'm out of the ball game."

On May 1, Babe Ruth, using the swing he copied from Joe Jackson, recorded his first home run as a Yankee. That day Brooklyn and Boston played the longest game in major league history, a 26-inning, 1–1 tie that lasted three hours and fifty minutes. Both pitchers, Leon Cadore of Brooklyn and Joe Oeschger of Boston, went the distance. The Brooklyn Robins (nicknamed after their manager, Wilbert Robinson), apparently not learning a lesson from the marathon game, played 13-inning and 19-inning games the following two days—and lost both of them. On May 14, Walter Johnson defeated the Detroit Tigers for his 300th career victory.

On May 20, with anti-gambling feeling running strong in Chicago, Cubs officials recruited policemen who disguised themselves as soldiers, bootblacks, and farmers. They mingled with fans in the bleachers while Grover Cleveland Alexander pitched against the Phillies. The police arrested two dozen fans for gambling. Alexander shut out Philadelphia, 3–0. But the loss did not affect Phillies manager Gavvy Cravath too much. His team was in the National League cellar. Besides, Cravath had other pressing concerns, like starting pitcher Lee Meadows every Saturday at home games. Meadows was one of the fastest workers in baseball and one way or another was done with his work quickly. This delighted Cravath and paved the way for the harried manager's early getaways to his weekend cottage.

The White Sox stumbled a bit in May from their blazing

early April getaway, and fell back a bit in the standings. It would not be until mid-August that they would be in the thick of a very tough pennant race.

On the first day of July, Walter Johnson of the Washington Senators pitched what would be the only no-hitter in major league baseball that 1920 season, nipping the Red Sox 1–0.

On July 15, Babe Ruth tied his season home run record of 29, hitting a 13th-inning shot against the St. Louis Browns. Two days later Ruth smashed two home runs off Dickie Kerr. During that series between the Yankees and White Sox, Babe Ruth presented Joe Jackson with one of his bats.

"Just promise me, kid," the Babe said, "that you won't use it against us." The bat weighed 50 ounces, a couple of ounces more than Black Betsy. Heeding Ruth's exhortation, Jackson used the bat infrequently. When he did, it was only as a kind of trigger for Black Betsy. By the end of July, the thirty-one-year-old Jackson was hitting nearly .400.

On August 16, 1920, the world of baseball was stunned by the news that submariner Carl Mays of the New York Yankees had hit Ray Chapman, the Cleveland Indians shortstop, in the head with a fastball.

A news account in the *Washington Star* reported the tragedy.

> So terrific was the blow that the report of impact caused spectators to think the ball had struck his bat. Mays . . . acting under this impression, fielded the ball which rebounded halfway to the pitcher's box, and threw it to first base to retire Chapman.

The next day the twenty-nine-year-old Chapman died—the only major leaguer to ever be killed in a game. Jackson and Chapman had been good friends years before in Cleveland. The news of the death upset Jackson. It also stirred rumblings throughout the American League that teams would not face Carl Mays, that they would boycott him whenever he pitched. Kid Gleason was contemptuous of all that kind of talk.

KID GLEASON: "The ballclub that determines not to play against Mays lacks courage. To me it appears as if they are afraid to oppose him. My ballclub does not look at it in that light. We will face Mays any and every time he pitches.

"We have never had any trouble with him. He has attempted to drive some of my players back from the plate when he thought they were getting a good toehold. That is part of the game. I used to do it. Therefore, I contend Mays hitting Chapman was accidental pure and simple, and there is no reason why any move should be made to boycott him."

The White Sox came into New York to play a three-game series and Mays was scheduled to pitch in the second game against Eddie Cicotte. Gleason and his "gang" went up against Mays without incident; there were those in the stands, though, who thought that some of the White Sox hitters were a little looser than usual in the batter's box. Neither Cicotte nor Mays were around at the finish as the Yankees won 6–5 in twelve innings.

Fans were coming out in record numbers to watch the tightest pennant race since 1908. The contenders were the Sox, who took over first place on August 21, seemingly in stride and charging after their second straight flag; the emerging powerhouse New York Yankees; and the Cleveland Indians, the sentimental favorite.

The only cloud on the blue baseball horizon was the rumors of sold and fixed games by players on the Yankees, Braves, Red Sox, Indians, Giants, and Cubs. In August, charges also began to surface that some White Sox players had engaged in game-selling that season, a practice not without precedent. Again talk of a fixed 1919 World Series was making the rounds.

On the next-to-last day of August the White Sox arrived in Boston for a three-game series. Their lead was a half game over the Indians. The Red Sox swept the series. It left the White Sox with a six-game losing streak and knocked them out of first place. In the Chicago-New York series the old animosity between Schalk and Cicotte, who blew a lead in the second game, flared up anew. A furious Eddie Collins also met with Comiskey and told him that the Boston series had been thrown. The Old Roman listened. That was all he did—listen.

The season moved into September; each play of each game was critical as the Yankees, White Sox, and Indians battled for the pennant.

Then on September 4, sports pages reported that on August 31 in Chicago, a fix had been arranged for the Phillies to defeat the Cubs. Chicago president William Veeck Sr. informed reporters that telephone calls and telegrams had alerted him to the fix. Veeck then arranged with Fred Mitchell, the Cubs manager, to have the team's stopper, Grover Cleveland Alexander, start out of his pitching turn. Despite the promise of a $500 bonus if he won, Alexander lost the game to the pathetic Phillies, who finished the season almost fifty games out of first. Although scheduled Chicago starting pitcher Claude Hendrix denied knowledge of a fix, 1920 was his last season in organized baseball. The Cubs released him during the offseason, and no other major league team signed him.

On September 7, a special Cook County Court Grand Jury was put in place to investigate that much-publicized August 31 Cubs-Phillies game. The presiding judge, Charles MacDonald, and Illinois State Attorney General Maclay Hoyne said the investigations would not only center on the Cubs-Phillies game, but on baseball gambling in general.

The Cook County Court Grand Jury hearings were held behind closed doors. Testimony came from a crazy quilt of characters—owners, players, managers, writers, odd men out. Newspaper accounts of what took place, analyses in books and articles, and quoted statements in a variety of printed sources— all vary in content and substance. The information that emerged was second-hand or hearsay or press conference pronouncements by individuals involved. In essence, coverage of the hearings can charitably be characterized as a journalistic free-for-all. Reporters of the time who cut their teeth on hearsay and hyperbole gorged themselves on the legalistic menu being served. Perhaps the most curious turn of events in all the tumult was that the avowed purpose of the hearings—the focus on the August 31 Cubs-Phillies game—was replaced by a probe into what happened or did not happen in the 1919 World Series.

Newspapers reported that Ban Johnson and Charles Comiskey, two of the first to testify, used their time in the judicial spotlight to go at each other. These two men, key figures in the founding of the American League, had once been hunting and fishing buddies. But that was in the past; now all that was left between them was animosity.

Comiskey declared he had heard rumors of shady dealings in the 1919 series. He had informed John Heydler of them and told Johnson, who refused to cooperate.

CHARLES COMISKEY: "I told Heydler that I was sending for him, and not for Johnson, because I had no confidence in Johnson. I employed a large force of detectives to run down every clue and paid them over $4,000 for their services."

BAN JOHNSON: "The result of such an alleged investigation has never been communicated to me, nor to the league."

Comiskey said he was so alarmed by all the rumors and charges that he had delayed mailing the World Series bonus checks of eight White Sox players.

CHARLES COMISKEY: "If any of my players are not honest, I'll fire them no matter who they are. If I can't get honest players to fill their places, I'll close the gates of the park that I have spent a lifetime to build and in which in the declining years of my life, I take the greatest measure of pride and pleasure."

On Tuesday, September 21, with two weeks left in the 1920 season, Cleveland defeated the Red Sox, 12–1, pushing its winning streak to seven games. Player-manager Tris Speaker, who would bat .388 that season, welcomed a day off. The Indians rested, awaiting a crucial three-game series against the White Sox at League Park. Chicago had won six straight games, and were only a game and a half behind. That off-day, a statement by Ban Johnson pushed the news of the pennant race aside.

BAN JOHNSON: "I have evidence and much of it now before the Grand Jury that certain notorious gamblers are threatening to expose the 1919 World Series as a fixed event unless the Chicago White Sox players drop out of the current race intentionally to let the Indians win. These gamblers have made heavy bets on the Indians."

CHARLES COMISKEY: "It was a terrible thing to report the blackmail of my players by gamblers just before they went into a series against Cleveland, a club in which Mr. Johnson has financial interests!"

In Cleveland, Kid Gleason left his hotel room and headed to League Park. Reporters trailed after him.

KID GLEASON: "I have nothing to say in the matter from any phase whatsoever except that we are trying our best to win the pennant, all reports to the contrary notwithstanding. I know nothing of the reports that my players were involved in a gambling plot to throw away any World Series."

TRIS SPEAKER: "Such reports are entirely new to me, and I don't take any stock in them. In this series here, two great ball teams are fighting as hard as they know how, with the honor of getting into the World Series as their stake. But the thing to do is to root out the baseball gambling that is responsible for all these stories. Suppress this evil and you'll kill off the thing that is now besmirching our great national game. That's the way to clean up all this mess of scandal."

The White Sox, behind Dickie Kerr, trimmed Cleveland 10–3 in the opener of the series, chopping the Indians lead to just a half-game.

John Walter Mails, an outspoken left-hander better known as Duster Mails, was tabbed by Cleveland manager Tris Speaker to start the second game. "I'm going to shut those bums out," Mails bragged to umpire Billy Evans.

"You mean you've never heard of Joe Jackson, Buck Weaver, and Eddie Collins?" the umpire asked.

"Sure, I have. But the question is have they ever heard of the Great Mails?"

Beginning the game throwing sidearm, Mails then switched to an overhand delivery; some of the Sox moaned about his contortionist pitching. True to his word, Mails hurled Cleveland to a 2–0 win, outpitching Red Faber. It was the only time

Mails ever faced Jackson, and he held him hitless. Mails won seven decisions without a loss that year.

In the final game of the series, Jackson more than made up for the Mails treatment. He slammed out three hits, one of them a booming fifth-inning homer off Stan Coveleski over the fence in right field. The home run, the final one of his career, boosted Jackson's batting average to .387. The White Sox racked up a 5–1 win and trailed the Indians by just a half-game. The two teams would battle in nip-and-tuck fashion through the remaining days of the schedule.

On September 27, the White Sox played the Tigers. Ty Cobb's batting average was down around .330, far behind that of George Sisler, Tris Speaker, Babe Ruth, Eddie Collins, and Joe Jackson. Dickie Kerr pitched the White Sox to a 2–0 victory. It would be the last major league game that Jackson, Weaver, Cicotte, Williams, Gandil, Felsch, and McMullin would ever suit up for.

That same day, a story exploded over baseball's landscape. GAMBLERS PROMISED WHITE SOX $100,000 TO LOSE was the headline in the *Philadelphia North-American*. The story beneath was an interview by James C. Isaminger with Bill Maharg, a small-time gambler, former boxer, and a man who had the briefest of tenure in the major leagues: one game for the 1912 Tigers and one game for the 1916 Phillies. Maharg told how in September 1919 he was contacted by William "Sleepy" Burns, who had once played for the Reds and the White Sox and then had gone on to make a small fortune in the Texas oil fields. Burns suggested they meet at the Ansonia Hotel in New York City to make arrangements to go hunting at his New Mexico ranch.

But the agenda at the Ansonia was gambling, not hunting. It was there, according to Maharg, that Burns introduced him to Ed Cicotte and Chick Gandil, who were in town to play the New York Yankees. Cicotte, Maharg reported, claimed that a group of prominent players on the White Sox would be willing to "throw" the World Series for $100,000. Maharg said he approached gamblers in Philadelphia; however, they were unable to come up with such a large sum. According to Maharg, they then suggested he make contact with Arnold Rothstein, the wealthy and well-known New York gambler.

"We [Burns and Maharg] met Rothstein by appointment at the Astor," the roly-poly Maharg said. "But Rothstein turned his back on the deal thinking that a fix of a World Series was not possible."

Upon returning to Philadelphia, Maharg said he received the following telegram from Burns:

"ARNOLD R HAS GONE THRU WITH EVERYTHING. GOT EIGHT IN. LEAVING FOR CINCINNATI AT 4:30."

When he arrived at the Hotel Sinton in Cincinnati, Maharg continued, he met with Burns, who told him that Rothstein "laid off us because he didn't know us but was very willing to talk turkey with Abe Attell who he knew."

Attell, former featherweight champion of the world, was, in Maharg's words, "quartered in a large suite in the Sinton and had a gang of about twenty-five New York gamblers with him. He said they were all working for Rothstein. Their work was very raw. They stood in the lobby of the Sinton and buttonholed everybody who came in. They accepted bets left and right, and it was nothing unusual to see $1,000 bills wagered."

Maharg said that he and Burns visited Attell on the morning of the first World Series game and asked for the $100,000 to give to the White Sox players to carry out "our part of the deal."

But according to Maharg, Attell refused to pass on the money. Instead, he promised to pay a sum of $20,000 after each White Sox defeat that was fixed. Burns, Maharg reported, went to the players with this proposition "and they seemed satisfied with the new arrangement." All bets were on Cincinnati in the first game; all the gamblers involved won.

BILL MAHARG: "The next morning Burns and I went around to Attell at his headquarters. I never saw so much money in my life. Stacks of bills were being counted on dressers and tables."

But according to Maharg, Attell once again refused to pay, which made him and Burns suspicious. They began to wonder if Arnold Rothstein was really in on the deal. At that point, Attell produced a telegram:

"ABE ATTELL, SINTON HOTEL, CINCINNATI HAVE WIRED YOU TWENTY GRAND AND WAIVED IDENTIFICATION."

BILL MAHARG: "The wire was signed with the initials 'A.R.' We learned later that was a fake telegram. . . . Rothstein was never involved. Attell was lying."

Ultimately, according to Maharg, the only money Attell handed over was $10,000 after the second game was lost. "The players were restless and wanted the full amount, Burns told me. He was afraid they would not keep up the agreement." Instead the players reassured Burns. They told him that if they had lost behind Cicotte and Lefty Williams, they certainly wouldn't win for Dickie Kerr, a rookie, a busher.

Assured and convinced, Burns and Maharg bet all their personal winnings from the first two games on Cincinnati to win the third game.

BILL MAHARG: "The Sox got even with us by winning that game. Burns and I lost every cent we had in our clothes. I had to hock my diamond pin to get back to Philadelphia. The whole upshot is that Attell and his gang cleaned up a fortune, and the Sox players were double-crossed out of $90,000 that was coming to them."

Although the comments of Maharg were those of an embittered small-time gambler who claimed he had been double-crossed and squeezed out of the profits, *The New York Times* labeled his story "one of the most amazing and tangled tales of graft and bribery and interlocking double-crossing."

Although virtually all of Maharg's knowledge of the inner doings and gambling machinations of the 1919 World Series ended after the third game, what he said set forces in motion that would affect lives, reputations, and fortunes.

Baseball executives talked of cancelling the 1920 World Series, of doing away with the 1921 season. But fans continued to vote with their feet, showing their disbelief in all the news of the scandal. With just a few days left in the 1920 season, a season that saw major league attendance top 9 million, up from the 6.5 million of the shortened 1919 season, fans were still filling Comiskey Park in record numbers.

The morning after Maharg's story appeared, Eddie Cicotte supposedly went to Comiskey's house and admitted to the Chicago owner that Maharg's story was basically correct and that he was one of the ring.

"I have played a crooked game," Cicotte reportedly said, "and I have lost." Acting like a benevolent uncle, Comiskey told Cicotte that his best course of action was to meet with his attorney.

Alfred Austrian was a Harvard graduate, a connoisseur of the arts, and a senior partner in the powerful and prestigious Chicago law firm of Mayer, Myer, Austrian, and Platt. He was also the attorney for Bill Veeck Sr. and the Chicago Cubs, and Charles Comiskey and the Chicago White Sox. But he never read the sports pages, cared very little for baseball, and looked at the teams he represented merely as corporate clients. When the 1919 World Series ended, Comiskey had conferred with him about confronting the players under suspicion. Austrian advised Comiskey to hire private detectives to look for hard evidence. Without hard evidence, the attorney reasoned, there would be no confessions.

Now he thought otherwise. At 11:30 A.M., followed by Cicotte, who was flanked by a pair of bailiffs, Alfred Austrian moved through a crush of spectators into the Criminal Courts Building. He introduced the pitcher to Assistant State's Attorney Hartley Replogle. Cicotte, nervous, visibly sweating, still could feel what it was like when he had signed a sheet of paper for Austrian earlier and could still hear Austrian's voice assuring him: "Don't worry. We will take care of you. Everything will be all right." The sheet of paper that Cicotte had signed was a waiver of immunity.

Once he had escorted Cicotte into the court, Austrian departed. He had, it seemed, other pressing matters.

Hundreds of streamer headlines would alliteratively capitalize on what happened next: CICOTTE CONFESSES . . . CICOTTE CONFESSES . . . CICOTTE CONFESSES.

Cicotte's purported Grand Jury testimony—which appeared in different versions with various embellishments in newspapers all over the country—focused on his need for money to pay off a mortgage on a farm, on his responsibilities to his wife and children. Reports said he admitted to purposely making a wild throw, to throwing the ball to the plate so "that you could have read the trademark on it," to intercepting Jackson's throw from the outfield that probably would have cut off a run. The only gamblers he named were Maharg and Burns. They had named him. He said Joe Jackson was one of the players involved in the fix. But, he admitted, his fingering of Jackson was not through any first-hand knowledge, but through word of mouth by Gandil, whom Cicotte tabbed "master of ceremonies."

On September 28, Jackson met with Austrian in a vacant office of the courthouse, naively assuming, like Cicotte, that Comiskey's lawyer would represent his own best interests. Austrian explained, in the tones of a teacher instructing a student, that Jackson owed it to himself and to baseball to testify. Jackson protested that he had not thrown games, that he had played his best.

Austrian countered that if the gamblers knew Jackson had not cooperated, they would be furious. "These men can be very dangerous. They have guns and all kinds of connections," he said. On the other hand, Jackson was so famous a player that he had nothing to worry about. "Mr. Comiskey will look out for you," Austrian reassured him.

Jackson persisted, complaining about the door that was slammed on him by Grabiner and how he was never given a chance to tell Charles Comiskey everything that he knew. But the lawyer argued it was not the players the court was concerned with, it was only the gamblers. "You're a witness," Austrian said, "you're not on trial." The forceful attorney convinced a reluctant Jackson to sign a paper he could not read—a waiver of immunity— and to testify before the Grand Jury.

Jackson began that morning by fortifying himself for what would undoubtedly be a trying day with a considerable amount of moonshine whiskey. About three in the afternoon he was escorted down the corridor to the Grand Jury Room. The walk was a crushing gauntlet of photographers, reporters, and bailiffs. Unshaven, bleary-eyed, smelling of alcohol, confused, and frightened, Jackson covered his face with his big hands against the flashing light bulbs, the barrage of reporters' questions, the badgering. Then he let go. All the frustration and anger, like pus pricked from a boil, rushed out in a stream of curses.

On the stand, Jackson responded in his slow southern drawl to two hours of questioning by Replogle. Authorities made sure evening newspapers had access to information in time to meet deadlines. "I am the left fielder for the Sox," he was quoted as testifying. "When a Cincinnati player would bat a ball out into my territory, I'd muff it if I could. But if it would look too much like crooked work to do that, I'd be slow and would make a throw to the infield that would be too short. My work netted the Cincinnati team several runs that they would never have made had I been playing on the square. I helped throw games by muffing hard chances in the outfield or by throwing slowly to the infield." A *Chicago Tribune* account related that Jackson admitted he and the others had tried their best to lose the third game but that Dickie Kerr won it anyway.

The actual records of the Grand Jury of Cook County of September 28, 1920, entitled "Into the Matter of the Investigation of Alleged Baseball Scandal," (see Appendix) contain no such confessions. Jackson admitted there was a plan to throw games for which he received $5,000 of the $20,000 promised and that he was ashamed and sorry he took the money. He described the arrangements and deals, the principals, the betrayals. While he said games were thrown, he insisted he did not make one intentional error during the whole Series, that he batted, ran, and fielded to win.

Later in life he related how he was "made bothered and confused during the investigation." Small wonder. An uneducated, illiterate, unsophisticated man, Jackson was not aware that his appearance as a suspected felon before a Grand Jury was highly irregular. He had no understanding of the principle of waiver of immunity. He didn't know that by signing the document fostered upon him by Austrian, he prepared the way for his own testimony to be used against himself. Moreover, he did not realize that both he and Cicotte were acting on the advice of counsel whose hidden agenda was to protect the client who paid his bills, namely Charles Comiskey.

Accompanied by two bailiffs, Jackson left the courthouse. The press of photographers and reporters and fans were on him.

First there was "Shoeless Joe." Now a second phrase was trotted out, to be forever fixed to the ballplayer's personage. In the *New York Evening World,* Hugh Fullerton evoked in epic language the country boy's fall from grace.

> From out of the hills of North Carolina years ago, there came a raw-boned, strong, active youth. His shoulders were broad and his body lithe and active. Some scout for the teams of organized baseball had discovered him up in the hills playing baseball. In two years he had risen from a poor mill boy to the rank of a player in the major leagues.
>
> The rumor went around the country that he had been found playing ball in his bare feet, and that it was with difficulty that the scout who hired him to play with a minor league club was forced to hog-tie him to get shoes on him, and that he had wailed that he couldn't hit unless he could get toe-holds.
>
> The story, perhaps, was untrue, but it survived, and its fame grew as the youth commenced to hit. In his first year in the big leagues as a member of the Cleveland club, he became one of the famous figures of the national sport. Of all the players in America, this boy had become one of the greatest. Each season, he and Ty Cobb battled for the honors of hitting and "Shoeless Joe" Jackson, the unknown, the rough, uncouth mill boy from the mountains, became one of the famous men of the United States. . . . He could not read nor write. . . . There came a day when a crook spread money

before this ignorant idol, and he fell. For a few dollars, which perhaps seemed a fortune to him, he sold his honor. And when the inevitable came, when the truth stood revealed, Joe Jackson went before a body of men and told the story of his own infamy.

While he related the sordid details to the stern-faced, shocked men, there gathered outside the big stone building a group of boys. Their faces were serious—more serious than those who listened inside to the shame of the nation's sport. There was no shouting, no scuffling. They did not talk of baseball or of anything else. A great fear and a great hope fought for mastery within each kid's heart. It couldn't be true.

After an hour, a man, guarded like a felon by other men, emerged from the door. He did not swagger. He slunk along between his guardians, and the kids with wide eyes and tightening throats watched. And one, bolder than the others, pressed forward and said:

"It ain't so Joe, is it?"

Jackson gulped back a sob. The shame of utter shame flushed his brown face. He choked an instant.

"Yes, kid, I'm afraid it is."

JOE JACKSON: "No such word 'Say it ain't so' was ever said. The fellow who wrote that just wanted something to say. When I came out of the courthouse that day, nobody said anything to me. The only one who spoke was a guy who yelled at his friend 'I told you the big son of a bitch wore shoes.' I walked right out of there and stepped into my car and drove off."

Despite Jackson's denial, Fullerton's purple prose simply perpetuated what has become part of American mythology. Chicago newsman Don M. Ewing claimed he'd heard the dialogue and written the original story, a sidebar to the trial report. In *Sport* magazine in 1949, Jackson offered yet another version of the "Say it ain't so, Joe" story:

JOE JACKSON: "I guess the biggest joke of all was that story that got out about 'Say it ain't so, Joe.' Charley Owens of the *Chicago Daily News* was responsible for that. There wasn't a bit of truth in it. . . .

"There weren't any words passed between anybody except me and a deputy sheriff. When I came out of the building, this deputy asked me where I was going, and I told him to the South Side. He asked me for a ride, and we got in the car together and left. There was a big crowd hanging around in front of the building, but nobody said anything to me. It just didn't happen. That's all. Charley Owens just made up a good story and wrote it. Oh, I would have said it ain't so, all right, just like I'm saying it now."

Lefty Williams, the third of the White Sox players to testify, provided information under some would say highly unusual circumstances. Alfred Austrian posed the questions, his staff recorded the answers, and the written record was given to the grand jury and reporters.

This account has Williams claiming that Gandil approached him at the Ansonia Hotel in New York with Burns's and Attell's offer of $100,000 for a World Series fix. Later in Chicago, he met with Cicotte, Gandil, Weaver, and Felsch at the Warner Hotel along with two gamblers: Rachael Brown and Joseph Sullivan (aka Nat Evans and Sport Sullivan). The gamblers reportedly offered $80,000 to eight players, including $10,000 for Williams to lose the second game. At the end of the fourth game, Gandil handed him $10,000 and said: "Five for you and five for Jackson. The rest has been called off." Williams also said that gamblers had told him that his wife would be killed if he didn't let down in the final game. Oddly, Austrian raised no question and Williams gave no information about the eighth game, which Williams pitched and lost.

Happy Felsch, who admitted receiving $5,000, unburdened himself to Chicago newspapermen:

"I'm not saying that I doublecrossed the gamblers but I had nothing to do with the loss of the World Series. The breaks just came so that I was not given a chance to do anything towards throwing the games . . . whether I could actually have gotten up nerve enough to carry out my part in throwing the games

I cannot say . . . The gold looked awfully good to all of us and I suppose I would have gone ahead with the double cross, but as I said I was given no chance to decide. . . . I'm as guilty as the rest," Felsch said, ". . . looks like the joke's on us, doesn't it."

With the signed testimony of Jackson and Cicotte in hand implicating their teammates Happy Felsch, Chick Gandil, Lefty Williams, Swede Risberg, Fred McMullin, and Buck Weaver, the Grand Jury acted. On September 28, it ordered indictments against all eight players, charging that they conspired to throw the 1919 World Series. The crime carried with it a penalty from one to five years in jail and/or a maximum fine of $10,000.

Closeted in his office at Comiskey Park, the sixty-year-old Charles Comiskey felt his age. The bigness of his body, the power of his influence, seemed to evaporate. So had his dream of the 1920 pennant for his beloved White Sox.

Slowly, carefully, he dictated identical telegrams to the eight indicted players:

"YOU AND EACH OF YOU ARE HEREBY NOTIFIED OF YOUR INDEFINITE SUSPENSION OF THE CHICAGO AMERICAN LEAGUE BASEBALL CLUB. YOUR SUSPENSION IS BROUGHT ABOUT BY INFORMATION WHICH HAS JUST COME TO ME, DIRECTLY INVOLVING YOU (AND EACH OF YOU) IN THE BASEBALL SCANDAL NOW BEING INVESTIGATED BY THE (PRESENT) GRAND JURY OF COOK COUNTY, RESULTING FROM THE WORLD SERIES OF 1919.

"IF YOU ARE INNOCENT OF ANY WRONGDOING, YOU AND EACH OF YOU WILL BE REINSTATED; IF YOU ARE GUILTY, YOU WILL BE RETIRED FROM ORGANIZED BASEBALL FOR THE REST OF YOUR LIVES IF I CAN AC-COMPLISH IT.

"UNTIL THERE IS A FINALITY TO THIS INVESTIGATION, IT IS DUE TO THE PUBLIC THAT I TAKE THIS ACTION EVEN THOUGH IT COSTS CHICAGO THE PENNANT."

Implicit in the wording of the telegram was Comiskey's feeling that the players would be exonerated in a court of law. Always one to keep his office door locked, now he left the door open for the return of the accused players, the nucleus of his powerhouse team.

COMISKEY: "Thank God it did happen. Forty-four years of

baseball endeavor have convinced me more than ever that it is a wonderful game and a game worth keeping clean."

The reactions to the Comiskey telegram and to the public disclosure of the fix ranged from outrage and disbelief to self-serving and face-saving commentaries.

Newsboys in Boston shouted out news of the "Benedict Arnolds of Baseball." In Joliet, Illinois, a crazed fan cursed Buck Herzog, calling him "one of the crooked Chicago ballplayers." The two got into a fight, and Herzog was stabbed several times. Herzog played for the Chicago Cubs, not the White Sox.

Aged Cap Anson blasted John Heydler and Ban Johnson, calling them weak-kneed and wondering aloud why the two league presidents hadn't stepped in to clean up the abuses "in the great game of baseball" instead of passing the buck to a grand jury.

BABE RUTH: "It was like hearing that my church had sold out."

COLONEL HUSTON: "This is a case of a sweet young lady turned whore."

Colonel Ruppert, who along with Colonel Huston owned the Yankees, went out of his way to show how much he cared for Comiskey and "his terrible sacrifice to preserve the integrity of the game." Rupert even went as far as offering the whole roster of the Yankees to Comiskey for the remainder of the season—even for the World Series if need be. And Red Sox owner Harry Frazee urged that each American League team "donate" one player to the White Sox as replacement for those suspended by Comiskey. Of course, according to baseball rules none of these gracious offers was possible. However, Ruppert and Frazee enjoyed good press as a result of their public pronouncements.

Back on the baseball field on the day of the indictments, Cleveland won again and moved its lead to a full game over the White Sox, who had two games left to play.

In downtown Chicago in a kind of mock celebration of the indictments of the newly named "Black Sox," the rest of the team now called the "Square Sox" had dinner. They commiserated with each other about the great load that had been lifted from them and talked to reporters about the code of silence that had been in operation all season between the accused and the honest players. "We went along and gritted our teeth and played ball," one of them said. "Now the load has been lifted. No wonder we feel like celebrating."

EDDIE COLLINS: "We've known there was something wrong for a long time, but we felt we had to keep silent because we were fighting for a pennant. . . . They were old enough to know the difference between right and wrong."

A front page story in *The Sporting News* noted that fans all over the country were amazed by revelations of the scandal:

> . . . but they didn't surprise the insiders who felt certain since last fall that something had been all wrong with the 1919 World Series. The confession of Eddie Cicotte, corroborated by Williams, Jackson and others turned up a trail in the direction of the crooked parasites who prey on professional sports and many of whom make New York their headquarters. . . .
>
> Comiskey had no alternative but to suspend his indicted players. He should have taken a step further by declaring his ball team out of the American League race, instead of permitting Gleason's men to jeopardize the chances of the Cleveland team.

The suspended Jackson was having a career year, batting .382, third behind Tris Speaker and George Sisler, who would win the title with a .407 average. He was third in slugging, total bases, doubles, and triples, fourth in runs batted in, and had hammered a dozen home runs, an indication of his power potential in the coming lively-ball era.

The revised Chicago lineup saw outfielder Shano Collins take over at third base. Harvey A. McClennan, a rarely used reserve, played shortstop. Eddie Collins was at second base and Ted Jourdan at first base. The revamped outfield comprised veterans Nemo Liebold, Amos Strunk, and Eddie Murphy. The pitching staff consisted of Kerr, Faber, Tex Wilkinson, and Shovel Hodge.

When Comiskey suspended the accused players, the White Sox were in a virtual tie with Cleveland for first place. The Indians won three of their last five games and clinched their first pennant after thirty-nine years of striving.

The *Cleveland Plain Dealer* showcased a front-page three-column illustration of an Indians player. He leaned on a bat and held his cap to his side. The player gazed at a giant pennant flapping on the horizon. Ray Chapman looked down from the clouds. Above him were the words "Carry on." The illustration was captioned, "It pays to play clean."

The Sporting News said: "The triumph of Cleveland is a triumph for honest ball and is hailed everywhere. Had the White Sox finished in front, the World Series would have been unpopular and farcical, and the game would have fallen deeper into the Slough of Despond."

The White Sox, with four 20-game winners—Williams, Cicotte, Urban Faber, and Dickie Kerr—wound up two games off the pace in second place, one game ahead of the New York Yankees.

The official final American League standings did not please many, including *The Sporting News*. "Every game played by the White Sox this year should be thrown out of the American League record," the baseball paper declared. "The team collectively should be disqualified in the World Series second place money inasmuch as the victories of the White Sox were dishonestly won. It is extremely unfair to deprive the Yankees of the second prize."

At that crossroads time for baseball and America, the New York Yankees of Babe Ruth were power personified. That 1920 season the Babe became the first player to crack the .800 slugging barrier, smashing the ball at an .847 clip, 99 of his 172 hits extra basers. He tallied 148 league-leading walks—more than one a game. He was on base 379 times in 1920, an all-time record. And he slammed an unprecedented 54 home runs, one every 11.8 times he came to bat. The persona of Babe Ruth helped to diffuse some of the sport's scandal. But the talk, the trauma, and the tensions created by the indictments of the White Sox players would not go away.

Major league owners, sensitized and stung by negative publicity, gathered to discuss ways to reform and make the game more modern. In one of their first meetings, on October 2, a day the first and last triple header of the twentieth century was played (between Pittsburgh and Cincinnati), Albert D. Lasker, a minority stockholder of the Cubs, proposed the creation of a three-member board of non-baseball men, to be headed by a chairman. Candidates mentioned for the chairman, who would be paid $25,000 a year, included former President William Howard Taft, General John J. Pershing, Senator Hiram Johnson, Judge Charles MacDonald, General Leonard Wood, former Secretary of the Treasury William McAdoo, and Judge Kenesaw Mountain Landis.

On the fifth day of October 1920, a month the great horse Man O' War won his final race, Cleveland faced Brooklyn at Ebbets Field in the first game of the best-of-nine format World Series. The Robins wore cream pinstriped uniforms. The Indians were dressed in their road grays and wore black mourning armbands on the left sleeve in memory of their slain teammate Ray Chapman.

On that raw day in Brooklyn, a subdued Eddie Collins was a forlorn figure, bundled up in a bulky overcoat like so many of the 23,573 fans at Ebbets Field. Earlier that day he had visited Cleveland players at the Pennsylvania Hotel in Manhattan and wished them the best of luck. Cleveland player-manager Tris Speaker, taking no chances on the whims of gamblers, waited until game time to name his starting pitcher that day and throughout the Series.

It turned out to be a Series of interesting firsts. Wheeler Johnson of Cleveland and Jimmy Johnson of Brooklyn became the first brothers to play against each other in a World Series. In Game Five Bill Wambsganss, Cleveland's second baseman, recorded the first unassisted triple play in World Series history.

BILL WAMBSGANSS: "The only thing anybody seems to remember is that I made an unassisted triple play in the Series . . . You'd think I was born the day before and died the day after."

Cleveland's Elmer Smith hit the first bases-loaded home run in World Series history; his teammate Jim Bagby recorded the first home run ever by a pitcher in a World Series. On the other hand, Robin pitcher Clarence Mitchell held the dubious distinction of hitting into a triple play and then into a double play. Cleveland defeated Brooklyn, five games to two. The victory was largely due to the pitching of future Hall of Famer Stan Coveleski, one of the "grandfathered" legal spitballers. Coveleski posted an earned run average of 0.67 and won three games.

Charles Comiskey, claiming he was touched by the valiant efforts of his "Square Sox" that 1920 season, presented a check for $1,500 to each of them. The White Sox players, equally touched, addressed an open letter to the fans of Chicago. "We the undersigned players of the Chicago White Sox want the world to know the generosity of our employer who of his own free will has reimbursed each and every member of our team the difference between the winning and losing share of last year's World Series, amounting to approximately $1,500."

The actual difference in shares was $1,952.71. Comiskey always had a way of balancing the books in his favor.

The 1920 World Series had ended. But news coming out of the courthouse in Chicago seemed to have no end in sight. The trial was stuck on front pages like a fly on flypaper in Texas in mid-August. The "Black Sox Scandal" was being dissected daily, and it would not go away. The indicted players were reamed and ragged daily in newspapers. Self-serving and ambitious politicians pontificated about the Sox at every available moment, grabbing headlines all over the country.

Cook County Attorney General MacClay Hoyne was a lame duck since he had been defeated in the Democratic primary prior to the hearings. On vacation in New York City, Hoyne saw his assistant Hartley Replogle garnering publicity. Not to be outdone, he declared the indictments would not stand up in a court of law; he was gathering new information, and the investigation should not be concluded until he returned to Chicago. In his opinion, it was doubtful that any crime was committed under the jurisdiction of the courts of Cook County. That set off a triple play: Judge MacDonald affirmed that the crime was covered by the law. *The New York Times* sided with Hoyne, claiming that the Attorney General should know what the law is; it then added that if the crime was not covered by law, it should be. Then Hoyne reversed himself and said that there was a law that covered the crime. Finally, the ambitious Replogle dredged up a suggestion already proffered by Ban Johnson that a federal statute should be passed that made throwing a baseball game a federal crime. It went on and on in the newspapers, in barrooms, barber shops, wherever people gathered—it was the talk of the time.

All kinds of talk were taking place in the Cook County Courthouse, where more and more witnesses were summoned to testify before the Grand Jury. The Halls of Justice became a circus for journalists, a nirvana for autograph-seekers, a nightmare for court stenographers.

Garry Herrmann testified. John J. McGraw testified. The "mystery woman," Mrs. Henrietta Kelly, testified. She owned a couple of houses near Comiskey Park and was Eddie Cicotte's landlady. She told the Grand Jury that after the Series ended, she overheard Cicotte say, "I don't care what happens. I got mine." Herrmann, McGraw, Mrs. Kelly, and others all had their moment in the media's glare.

But it was Joe Gedeon, who had batted .292 for the Browns in 153 games in 1920, who received the full Grand Jury spotlight treatment. Gedeon testified that he and fellow major leaguer Hal Chase—whom many thought was a behind-the-scenes figure in the fix, bet money on the Reds on a tip from Swede Risberg and won $600. He insisted, though, he had no idea at the start that the Series were going to be thrown. Gedeon revealed the existence of another group of gamblers involved in the fix, a group that included a St. Louis blouse manufacturer named Carl Zork, who was Abe Attell's ex-manager. The St. Louis connection also included Harry Redmon, a theater operator.

Redmon testified that he was present at a meeting where Zork spoke of the fix. A few weeks after the Series ended, Redmon said, he had passed on what he had heard to Kid Gleason. He was invited to Chicago where he met with Comiskey, Grabiner, and Austrian. But, Redmon claimed, none of them had been willing to do anything about what he told them. In fact, Redmon said, a testy Comiskey snapped that the "players had cost him a lot of money."

Harry Grabiner called Redmon's story "the hard-luck tale of a loser, but still every effort was made to verify his hearsay reports, but none was obtained until the deliberations of the Grand Jury brought out the confessions."

A badgered Comiskey went on the offensive. Claiming he had paid Redmon's expenses for his trip to Chicago as well as his purported loss, Comiskey called Redmon's charges "hearsay." "No one," the White Sox owner said, "would have been justified in taking affirmative action such as would destroy the character and reputation of men even though they were ballplayers." Then seeking further ammunition to denigrate Redmon, Comiskey disclosed that Ban Johnson had met with Redmon and had reached the same conclusion about the St. Louis theater operator.

Grabiner's tart comments and Comiskey's attempt to slough off Redmon's charges notwithstanding, the theater owner's testimony cast Comiskey in a negative light and stirred up yet more controversy. Newspapers claimed the White Sox owner was delinquent in his duty to act against the accused players. *The Sporting News* labeled him an owner who protected his investment "at the expense of the public."

Although indictments were handed down in September, the Cook County Grand Jury hearings continued through October. Daily newspaper reports described strange and strained alliances, bickering, backstabbing, and recriminations.

Sport Sullivan made public his rage at being named in the confession of Lefty Williams.

SPORT SULLIVAN: "They have made me a goat . . . and I'm not going to stand for it. . . . I know the big man whose money it was that paid off the Sox players—and I'm going to name him."

An infuriated Abe Attell vented his anger over the fact that he was the focus in the Maharg story.

ABE ATTELL: "It looks to me that Rothstein is behind these stories. I am surprised because I have been a good friend of his. He is simply trying to pass the buck to me. It won't go. . . . Rothstein is trying to whitewash himself. . . . I will shoot the lid sky high."

The testimony of Sport Sullivan and Abe Attell flushed thirty-eight-year-old Arnold Rothstein out and on to center stage. Once described as a "man willing to bet on anything except the weather because he cannot fix it," the New York City gambler showed up as a voluntary witness before the Grand Jury. Rothstein was represented by William J. Fallon, the man they called "the Great Mouthpiece," a skilled attorney known for his knack in bribing jurors and for his friendship with underworld figures.

Upon his arrival in Chicago, Rothstein called a press conference. He declared his love of baseball and described his friendship with the high and mighty of the national pastime. Rothstein was, in fact, connected in business dealings with Charles Stoneham, owner of the Giants, and for a time was a partner of John J. McGraw's in a poolroom operation. Blasting Attell and "other cheap gamblers" who had "framed the Series," an indignant Rothstein claimed he had "turned them down flat." Then he went off on an ironic tangent about how he did not deserve the notoriety that attached itself to him as he had long ago renounced gambling and now had an honest career in real estate.

ARNOLD ROTHSTEIN: "Gentlemen, what kind of a country is this? I came here voluntarily and what happens? A gang of thugs bars my path with cameras as though I was a notorious person—a criminal even! I'm entitled to an apology. I demand one! Such a thing couldn't happen in New York. I'm surprised at you!"

There was no short supply of surprise in the character references Rothstein amassed during his Chicago visit. District Attorney Hoyne said he did not believe that Rothstein had any involvement in the matter being investigated. Alfred Austrian said Rothstein proved himself "guiltless" in his appearance before the Grand Jury. Ban Johnson explained that he had conducted an interview with Rothstein in New York City and determined that although Rothstein knew about a fix, he was not a part of it.

Rothstein's appearance before the Grand Jury sent Abe Attell, Sport Sullivan, and Billy Maharg scurrying about like rats jumping off a sinking ship. Attell fled to Montreal. Sport Sullivan vanished from the country. Maharg declined to accept the $10,000 reward offered by Comiskey and became strangely silent.

Finally, on October 22, the Grand Jury hearings concluded. Judge Charles MacDonald, reminded by Ban Johnson that he was under consideration for the post of the new baseball commissioner position that was going to be created, moved swiftly. On November 6, 1920, four days after Warren Harding's landslide presidential victory, Judge MacDonald announced his decision.

> There is no question but what this injured and ruined the business of Mr. Comiskey as well as the honest players on the team, who would have obtained sixty percent of the players' share of the receipts instead of 40, if their team had won. There need be no doubt about the prosecution of the guilty players and their co-conspirators. None of these who have confessed has been granted immunity; in fact, each has specifically waived it. Of course, it will be natural for the prosecution to take into consideration service which the indicted have performed for the State, but that does not mean they will escape indictment.

> The legal proposition is sound. These men hatched a conspiracy . . . to throw the world's series and did 'throw' it. In so doing, they not only obtained money under false pretenses from Charles Comiskey, owner of the team, but they victimized their teammates out of . . . the extra amount which they would have shared if the White Sox had won the Series.

In addition to the eight White Sox players—Ed Cicotte, Claude Williams, Chick Gandil, Swede Risberg, Buck Weaver, Happy Felsch, Fred McMullin, and Joe Jackson—indictments would be handed down against Hal Chase, Abe Attell, Sport Sullivan, Sleepy Bill Burns, Nat Evans, and Rachael Brown, who was identified as a "steerer for Rothstein." Indictments were later handed down against St. Louis gamblers Carl Zork and Ben Franklin, and Attell's assistant David Zelser (aka Bennett) and his henchmen the Levi brothers.

The name of the man they called the "Big Bankroll" was conspicuously absent from the list. With all that he had going for him past and present, it was not surprising that Arnold Rothstein was exonerated "completely from complicity in the conspiracy." And a little whipped cream was added to his cake when several of the Grand Jury members pointed out that his testimony had strengthened the case against some of the defendants.

The indictments stunned the baseball community. Headlines in newspapers all over the United States ran the story in big, black, bold print:

GRAND JURY HAS YET TO REACH BIG MEN IN GAME'S SCANDAL

MEN ON INSIDE KNEW IT WOULD COME OUT

SHIFTY AS ATTELL IS HE CAN HARDLY SIDE-STEP THIS ONE

Nelson Algren, who would go on to gain international fame as a novelist, was then a boy on the South Side of Chicago. He idolized Swede Risberg. This emotional entanglement with the accused player caused Algren to become embroiled in several street battles in the months following the indictments. The Boston newsboys' club passed a resolution that condemned what they called "a murderous blow at the kid's game" struck by "the Benedict Arnolds of baseball." The *Philadelphia Bulletin* compared the indicted players with the "soldier or sailor who would sell out his country and its flag in time of war."

Once the pride of Chicago, the eight White Sox players were now in disgrace. Perhaps the least articulate, definitely the most introverted, Joe Jackson spent a lot of time waiting around in his Chicago apartment for the trial to begin. He and the other indicted players were under court order not to leave Illinois. Not being paid by the White Sox, Jackson drank even more than usual to ease the pain of his predicament. He had played baseball for so long and so well that he pondered what he would do without it. He opened a combination sports center and poolroom at 55th and Woodlawn across from the University of Chicago. "I got a lot of business from the University students," Jackson said later. And there were those who went home and bragged, "I played pool with Joe Jackson today."

The accused White Sox players were in limbo. But major league baseball was in turmoil. Club owners, reeling from recent battles against the challenge of the Federal League, negative publicity from World War I, and now the "Black Sox" scandal, reached for a face-saving device. They realized that for the game to survive, it was imperative to show the world that baseball was cleaning up its act. The National Commission, the three-man ruling body of baseball, would be abolished. The Lasker Plan—a chairman heading up a three-member board of non-baseball men—was shelved. That left one option. The hiring of a strong man, a commissioner to set the game back on course, was now on the table. Ban Johnson, often inebriated, often battling with one club owner or another, was violently opposed to the idea.

Bitter infighting began. Only five American League team owners—Philadelphia, Cleveland, St. Louis, Detroit, and Washington—supported Johnson. He called them the "Loyal Five." Others called them the "Willful Five." National League President Heydler and William Wrigley, owner of the Cubs, opposed Johnson. So did Comiskey, Ruppert and Hutson of the Yankees, Harry Frazee of the Red Sox, and every National League team owner.

HARRY FRAZEE: "If you [Johnson] had any sense of justice or realization of the harm you have caused baseball, or one spark of manhood, or any regard for the game which has made you possible, you would tender your resignation."

The New York Times echoed Frazee's harsh words: "The obstacle to reorganization is Ban Johnson, once a brilliant and successful executive, who now seems to think that baseball exists for his own greater glory . . . he would rather ruin a business than lose his job."

All the squabbling and animosity finally ran its course when the owners decided on the man they wanted: Federal Judge Kenesaw Mountain Landis.

Born in 1866 in Milville, Ohio, and named by his father after a Civil War battlefield (misspelled; Kennesaw was the correct spelling), Landis was a semi-educated lawyer. Andrew Jackson was one of his heroes, and it was said he looked like him. His craggy face, his thin and angular body, his white mane of shaggy hair and Lincolnlike chin beard projected probity and seriousness with a gothic touch. But it was all image.

In 1905, Landis's political connections clinched his appointment as Judge to the U.S. District Court for the Northern District of Illinois. Two years later, he made national headlines by fining Standard Oil $29,000,000 in an antitrust suit. That decision was later overturned. He also handled the sedition trial of International Workers of the World organizer Big Bill Haywood and gave him twenty-nine years. That decision, too, was later overturned. In fact, many of the judicial headlines garnered by K.M. Landis were ultimately overturned.

On November 12, 1920, all the major league owners gathered in Chicago to officially select a commissioner. Ban Johnson protested the appointment, claiming that Landis was a posing fraud. He argued that baseball should not bring in an outsider and that it should clean its own house.

But it was eleven teams versus five, and the eleven were in

earnest when they said they were ready to form a new major league if the five did not go along with their plan to hire Landis.

When the vote was taken, only Phil Ball, a rabid Ban Johnson loyalist and owner of the St. Louis Browns, abstained. All the others went along. Owners and their representatives piled into taxicabs and drove to the Federal Building to meet with the man who was known as "Integrity Mountain."

Landis was sitting in judgment on a case concerning $15,000 bribery on income tax fraud. In black robes, a profusion of silver hair, a stern visage, Landis utilized all of his props to full effect while he made the magnates stand and wait in silence.

HEYWOOD BROUN, writer: "He typified the heights to which dramatic talent may carry a man in America if only he has the foresight not to go on the stage."

Finally, the owners had their chance. Assembling with him in his private chambers, they proffered a $50,000-a-year offer to the judge to become Commissioner of Baseball. Landis accepted on unconditional terms: "The authority to do anything I consider right in any matter detrimental to baseball. . . . Neither faults in the law, miscarriages in the courts, or complaisance of magnates will prevent me from taking action in every case where I feel there was wrongdoing."

Though Landis was arbitrary, anti-minority, anti-immigrant, anti-union, anti-women, anti-nonwhite, and anti what he called "sissies"—to him, all those who were interested in things cultural—his image was one of honesty and toughness, and that was what the owners wanted. He also had a track record of siding with management against labor when it came to a showdown. That was what the owners wanted as well.

Ban Johnson did not get what he wanted. Reduced from his role as baseball's most powerful figure to that of supervisor of umpires and schedulemaker, Johnson nevertheless spoke the right words in defeat: "I am for Judge Landis, and I think the club owners acted wisely." The chastened American League president also made it clear that there would be "no more fights."

Noting that "fans emitted a huge sigh of relief," *The New York Times* dubbed the unanimous choice of Landis as "fortunate," an opinion not shared by all.

WILL ROGERS: "Baseball needed a touch of class and distinction. So somebody said, 'Get that old boy who sits behind first base all the time. He's out there everyday anyhow.' So they offered him a season's pass and he jumped at it. But don't kid yourself that the old judicial bird isn't going to make those baseball birds walk the chalk line."

JOHN DOS PASSOS, writer: "The judge could hand out twenty-five-year sentences as lightheartedly as he'd fine some Joe five bucks for speeding. . . . Underneath he was a butcher. . . . How could a man live with himself after doing what Kenesaw Mountain Landis did to men's lives for just saying a few illegal words? He throve on it."

The first few months of the Landis tenure as commissioner were unsettling. Always one to have his own way, always one to go out of his way to make an extra dollar, Landis insisted on being allowed to retain his federal bench position. Thus he drew two salaries. But not-so-gentle pressure from baseball executives and federal authorities finally convinced him to concentrate solely on his role as baseball commissioner. Landis, in fact, concentrated so zealously that two Congressmen tried to impeach him for "lobbying state legislatures" on behalf of baseball. It never reached the impeachment stage, but the intimidation was one of the main reasons he would retire from the bench in March 1922.

As 1920 came to an end, baseball's honeymoon with its new Commissioner was an ardent affair. Landis saw to that with frequent public pronouncements. "The only thing in anybody's mind now is to make baseball what the millions of fans throughout the United States want it to be," he declared, adding, "If I catch any crook in baseball the rest of his life is going to be a hot one."

He was not loathe to reveal his assumption of the roles of

judge, jury, and jailer, nor his prejudice and unbridled subjectivity to the whole complex and confusing case of the accused White Sox players.

JUDGE LANDIS: "There is absolutely no chance for any of them to creep back into Organized Baseball. They will be and will remain outlaws. . . . It is sure that the guilt of some of them will at least be proved."

8

1921

The plan was for the arraignment of the accused White Sox players to get under way in early February so that the trial could be completed in sufficient time for the players, should they be acquitted, to return to playing baseball. But things did not work out as planned.

On February 14, the chief prosecutor, former Congressman George Gorman, issued a shocking statement. The Grand Jury records, including the confessions of Cicotte, Williams, and Jackson, had disappeared. Turmoil and tumult took center stage as speculation abounded.

There was suspicion that either Maclay Hoyne, outgoing District Attorney, or his assistant, Hartley Replogle, had made off with the records and confessions. Hoyne had lost an election to Robert Crowe, an adept lawyer who would nevertheless meet his match in Clarence Darrow in the Leopold and Loeb case. There was also suspicion that Alfred Austrian was behind the thefts. Gorman, frustrated and beleaguered, said that he had no case. He would be unable to come up with new evidence before the trial deadline of March 14.

With the records missing and the players having filed affidavits repudiating their confessions, District Attorney Robert Crowe realized he had no choice but to offer a motion of *nolle prosequi,* an indication of unwillingness to prosecute. He would forego prosecution for the present in order to gain time to rebuild his case and secure new indictments. The action pleased the battery of brilliant defense attorneys.

The idle players, not drawing any paychecks and forced to wait while a new date was scheduled for the trial, attempted to capitalize on the fame, some would say notoriety, thrust upon them. Only Buck Weaver did not participate. He consciously sought to disassociate himself from the others.

Billing themselves the "Black Sox," the players scheduled an exhibition game at Murley Park in Chicago against the Aristo Giants. That triggered an emergency meeting of the directors of the Chicago Baseball League. "We have to protect the innocent from being soiled by the outlaws," said one director. Members of the Aristo Giants squad were advised that if they played against the Black Sox, they too would be banned from organized baseball. The Commonwealth Edison Company, owners of Murley Park, told the manager of the Aristo team that its facility was off limits. Then the Umpires' Protective League barred its members from working "any game of this type."

That game was never played, but there were quite a few others that were. Despite the orders served on the accused players not to leave Illinois, they managed individually or collectively to pick up a payday here and there playing a game of baseball.

JOE JACKSON: "I sneaked out of Illinois now and then to play with semipro teams in Indiana and Wisconsin. I always asked my lawyer Mr. Benedictine Short first, and he told me to go if I could get that kind of money."

Chicago broker George Miller raised some money and, christening the players the "Major Stars," put them on the road. He booked them wherever a pickup game could be arranged. But the National Baseball Federation issued orders blocking its teams from competing against the Black Sox.

Judge William E. Dever ordered the state's attorney to initiate extradition proceedings against any of the defendants who had left Illinois to avoid being brought to justice. Dever's action spurred renewed interest in the trial.

On March 12, 1921, Judge Landis placed the eight accused players on his "ineligible list." He reasoned that regardless of the twists and turns in the court, his action gave baseball a mechanism with which to protect itself.

Comiskey, though displeased by the turn of events, went along with them. Although he had suspended the accused players, he had retained them on his team's reserve list. Now his hand was being forced by Landis. He sent a formal notice to each of the eight players informing them of their release, and the termination of their contracts with the White Sox.

CHARLES COMISKEY: "Those players are on my ineligible list. There is absolutely no chance for them to play on my team again unless they can clear themselves to my satisfaction of the charges made against them by three of their teammates."

Ban Johnson now stepped into the picture, driven by his animosity towards Charles Comiskey, the legalistic foot-dragging, and the existence of new indictments albeit without any new evidence. Fearing that the players would never be brought to trial and that the Old Roman would wind up smelling like a rose, an irritated Johnson used his own money and American League funds to locate witnesses.

BAN JOHNSON: "I believe that all the guilty ones, players and gamblers, will be dealt with severely. A term of imprisonment would not surprise me at all."

Johnson managed to track down Bill "Sleepy" Burns in a Texas fishing village on the Rio Grande. In the middle of the night, Burns was briefed on the implications of his giving evidence—chief among them the assurance that he would be free from prosecution. In addition to the promise of immunity in exchange for turning state's evidence, Burns was given $500 in expense money. He accompanied the American League president back to Chicago.

Amid all the legal machinations, and the wheeling and dealing of personalities, the 1921 baseball season finally got under way. The chief emotion felt by major league club owners was trepidation. It was the first season since the scandal had broken. Once again, fears of fans staying away were misplaced.

More than 160,000 thronged into ballparks on Opening Day, and two attendance records were broken. Some of the owners bragged about the "comeback of baseball." A New York City sportswriter of the time was especially carried away by the moment. "The baseball season of 1921," he wrote, "burst into being, full-panoplied like Minerva emerging from the cracked brow of Jove, yesterday afternoon at the Polo Grounds."

On Opening Day at Comiskey Park 25,000 fans cheered the "darned but clean" White Sox. They outscored Detroit, 8–3. But one game did not make a season, and 1921 would be a long season for the White Sox: a collection of college kids, some not-prime-time minor leaguers, carryovers from 1920, and a few established stars. Over the winter Comiskey had purchased three-quarters of an infield from Salt Lake City: Ernie Johnson, Eddie Mulligan, and ponderously slow slugger Earl Sheely. In early March, Comiskey had traded Shano Collins and Nemo Leibold to the Red Sox for the steady .300 hitter Harry Hooper. Though Red Faber had 14 wins by June 17, the best the White Sox would manage was a seventh-place finish, 36½ games behind the pennant-winning New York Yankees.

The world champion Cleveland Indians were anxious to prove that their 1920 triumph was more than a fluke. Driven by Tris Speaker, Cleveland jumped out to a quick lead in the American League pennant race. The New York Yankees were close on their heels, powered by Babe Ruth. On May 7, the barrel-chested slugger smashed his eighth home run, the longest shot ever hit in Washington. Ruth's victim was Walter Johnson.

On June 27 the "Black Sox" trial finally got under way in Chicago before presiding Judge Hugo Friend. Notable absentees included Fred McMullin, who was not re-indicted for lack of evidence, Hal Chase, Joseph Sullivan, and Rachael Brown. Abe Attell was absent on a *habeas corpus* writ—a legal maneuver based on a bit of hocus pocus. The one-time featherweight champion had taken the witness stand before Supreme Court Justice Tierney in New York a month before and had sworn under oath that he was not the Abe Attell named in the indictments, that he knew none of the players, and that he had no part in the alleged fixing.

Throughout the trial, and despite the summer heat, the Cook County courtroom was packed to its capacity of five hundred. Many small boys were present. Special guards were hired to fend away all those who space could not accommodate.

More than 600 veniremen were involved in the jury selection, which took eight days. During the jury selection, Chicago White Sox manager Kid Gleason and several of the "Clean Sox" appeared in the courtroom. They commiserated with the defendants during a recess. Many were puzzled by the turnaround behavior exhibited by the "Clean Sox" to the "Black Sox." But later, Kid Gleason went out of his way to tell reporters that their visit was not designed to show support for the accused. The twists and turns did not stop.

Gorman was supported by two assistant district attorneys in his efforts for the prosecution. Apparently Ban Johnson did not think much of the support they gave nor the zealousness displayed by Gorman. So Johnson hired two "special prosecutors" to assist Gorman. At that time, interested third parties were permitted to employ attorneys to assist in the prosecution of their cases.

One of the special prosecutors was James G. "Ropes" O'Brien, a man who earned his nickname from his success in obtaining convictions and hangings. The other was George Barrett, a highly respected former judge.

Alfred Austrian's public connection with the accused players was severed as the trial moved into high gear. But his feverish behind-the-scenes activity was obvious: Comiskey's "Black Sox" were represented by an all-star team of legal minds, the best attorneys money could buy. And there were dozens of them at work.

One of the heavy hitters was Michael Ahearn, Al Capone's favorite lawyer. Ahearn and his partner Thomas Nash, who became a power broker in Chicago politics, were the attorneys for Swede Risberg, Happy Felsch, and Buck Weaver. Joe Jackson and Lefty Williams were represented by the brilliant former state's attorney Ben Short. Chick Gandil had "Ropes" O'Brien in his corner as the trial got under way. O'Brien was a lawyer on Comiskey's staff; he later switched sides. And where did the money come from to pay for this glittering array of defense counsel? Word was out that it came from the coffers of Charles Comiskey, hungering to get his stars back in uniform.

The case opened with a statement by the District Attorney that the original Grand Jury testimony (since retracted) and immunity waivers had been stolen. Ban Johnson charged that Arnold Rothstein had paid $10,000 to have the "confessions" stolen and that after seeing that he was not implicated by them, turned them over to a newspaperman. The missing evidence initiated a lively debate in baseball jargon about whether unsigned carbon copies of the confessions would be sufficient.

Ahearn: "You won't get to first base with those confessions."

Gorman: "We'll make a home run with them."

Ahearn: "You may make a long hit, but you'll be thrown out at home plate."

Such exchanges coupled with cries of fans like "attaboy" and "that's one for our side" created an atmosphere reminiscent of a baseball game. So bemused was Buck Weaver that he cracked, "They oughta build bleachers right here and charge admission."

The accused players sat in little clusters, mirror images of the cliques they had been part of as members of the White Sox. Buck Weaver was by himself, consciously avoiding eye contact with the others. Chick Gandil was also by himself. Swede Risberg and Happy Felsch sat close together. And Ed Cicotte, Lefty Williams, and Joe Jackson formed still another self-contained pocket.

Looking uncomfortable in a dark suit and smart tie, Joe Jackson was the odd man out. The trial would drag through the golden days of summer—baseball days. And he would sit there stuck indoors listening to the interminable monologues, the polysyllabic language, the short bursts and long barrages of verbiage of attorneys attempting to make their points. He probably comprehended only dimly what the words meant, what the score was as the ebb and flow of the judicial battles dragged on. When reporters asked Jackson what he thought of the whole scene, he was able to rise to the occasion and respond with good copy:

JOE JACKSON: "Those are certainly smart men. And that lawyer of mine is one lawyin' bird. They better not get him riled up."

In the witness chair under questioning by Ben Short, Jackson told how he had been promised that he could go anywhere, "all the way to the Portuguese Islands," and how he signed the immunity waiver not knowing what it was—"I'd have signed my death warrant if they asked me to."

Repeatedly he affirmed his innocence of any crime. He related how a week before the Series began he was offered a bribe to throw the Series and threatened to throw the unidentified man out of his hotel room. "And there were three other witnesses in the room," Jackson said. The identities of these witnesses were never revealed.

On July 5, a defense motion to dismiss the case was denied by the court.

Two of the most conflicting personalities in the courtroom were Jackson's defense attorney, Ben Short, and Bill Burns, the key witness for the prosecution. They got off some zingers at each other.

BEN SHORT: "You don't like me much, do you Bill?"

BILL BURNS: "Sure I like you, Ben. You're a smart fellow. I wish we had someone like you at the head of this deal. We'd all be rich now."

Despite the turncoat status of Burns, his only self-damaging admission was that Ban Johnson provided him with $500 for two months' living expenses. Surprisingly effective on both direct and cross examination, Burns placed every accused player at a meeting in the Hotel Sinton in Cincinnati prior to the first game with the exception of Jackson who, Burns believed, was represented by Lefty Williams.

Identifying Arnold Rothstein and Abe Attell as the money men behind the plot, Burns said they were committed to paying $100,000 to the players. He added that the plan was to have the first two games of the Series thrown. The order of the other fixed games would be open to discussion.

Although the 1919 Grand Jury confessions of Jackson, Cicotte, and Williams were nowhere to be found, the prosecution moved to allow court "reporters" to testify from their notes. Claiming waivers of immunity were signed involuntarily, the defense objected. Their objection was overruled by Judge Friend, who instructed the jury that it should not consider the confessions as evidence against the other players. Then he allowed court reporters to read the full texts of the confessions from their stenographic notes.

The much ballyhood and sought-after confessions proved to be tame evidence for the prosecution. There were admissions of consorting with gamblers to dump games and to take money. It was revealed that Cicotte received $10,000 even before he pitched Game One, and that Williams and Jackson each received $5,000 after the fourth game. However, all three players affirmed they had played to win, and it was this argument that was the most damaging to the prosecution. In effect, the only real evidence of actions in a conspiracy was that three players did accept money.

The defense's case was full of surprises. It trotted out manager Kid Gleason, catcher Ray Schalk, captain Eddie Collins, and other "Clean Sox" players. The appearance of Gleason and Schalk was especially unexpected. The White Sox manager had made public his suspicions about a fix throughout the Series. And Schalk had gone on record bragging that he was ready to give incriminating evidence, that he was going to tell how after the second game of the Series, he verbally and physically assaulted Lefty Williams. Yet now, both men testified for the defense.

Gleason and the other White Sox players appearing for the defense repudiated the testimony of Bill Burns and his claim of the meeting to set up the fix at the Sinton Hotel. All of them testified that the entire team was engaged in a practice session at that time.

Pandemonium prevailed in the courtroom when the defense counsel posed the following loaded question to each of the "Clean Sox":

"In your opinion, did the defendants play to the best of their abilities in the 1919 World Series?"

Strenuous objections to the question were raised by the prosecution. The objections were sustained by Judge Friend. He ruled that any answers to the question would be inadmissible.

It is clear, however, that defense counsel would never have raised the questions if they feared a negative response. It is also clear that Gleason and the "Clean Sox" took the stand to help acquit the defendants and enable them to return to play for the White Sox. And it is apparent that the actions of Gleason and the "Clean Sox" came with the blessings and backing of Charles Comiskey. The White Sox owner, of course, had a vested interest in acquittal.

As Illinois had no sports bribery statute, all the defendants could be convicted of was breach of contract with Comiskey and the White Sox baseball team. But the prosecution went down an ingenious route, demanding in its summary five-year jail sentences and a fine of $2,000 for each of the accused. It claimed a "swindle and con-game has been worked on the American people . . . the crime strikes at the heart of every red-blooded citizen and every kid who plays on a sandlot."

Defense attorney Ben Short, however, expressed the more popular view. "The magnates led the public to believe the ball-players got about $10,000 a year," he said, "and here we find out they got as little as $2,600. At the end of the season they have nothing left but a chew of tobacco, a glove and a few pairs of worn-out socks." Short charged that the prosecution was attempting to "make goats of underpaid ballplayers and penny-ante gamblers" while, at the same time, allowing such as Arnold Rothstein, Hal Chase, Abe Attell, and Bill Burns to escape the scales of justice.

Attorney Henry A. Berger led the efforts of the defense throughout the trial. He repeatedly charged that the prosecution of the case was inspired by Ban Johnson's self-serving motives and his desire to destroy Charles Comiskey. Berger's final argument asked for "complete vindication of the most mistreated ballplayers in history."

In his final instructions to the jury, Judge Friend sided with Berger and the defendants. "The state must prove," he said, "that it was the intent of the ballplayers and the gamblers charged with conspiracy through the throwing of the World Series to defraud the public and others and not merely to throw ballgames." The subtext of the judge's remarks indicated that he believed existing law was virtually inadequate as a means of punishing the alleged offense of the accused. Friend also said that on the basis of the evidence against Buck Weaver and Happy Felsch, he would not allow a verdict against them to stand.

It took just one ballot and two hours and forty-seven minutes that evening of August 2 for the jury to deliberate. All seven defendants as well as the gamblers David Zelser and Carl Zork were acquitted. (Indictments and cases against the other accused had been thrown out earlier.)

The not-guilty verdict, rendered largely as a result of the lack of hard evidence and the missing confessions, was greeted with cheers by the several hundred spectators along with cries of "Hooray for the Clean Sox." Popping flashbulbs punctuated the wild scene. Hats and papers were tossed high in the air. The bailiffs pounded for order, but then, noticing Judge Friend's smiling face, they too joined in the whistling and cheering.

Judge Friend congratulated the jury on what he called a fair decision. Buck Weaver and Swede Risberg were the most visibly affected by the verdict. Grabbing each other by the arms, they shouted out their thanks. Williams and Felsch just smiled. A subdued Jackson took the decision with very little emotion. Eddie Cicotte, the first of the defendants to reach the jurors, grabbed foreman William Barrett with both hands and shouted out his thanks. Joe Jackson and Lefty Williams were close on Cicotte's heels and shook hands with all the jurors.

Amid the pandemonium, Chick Gandil spotted Ban Johnson and snapped, "Goodbye, good luck, and to hell with you." And then he told onlookers: "I guess that will learn Ban Johnson that he can't frame an honest bunch of players." A smiling Buck Weaver told reporters, "I knew I'd be cleared and I'm glad the public stood by me until the trial was over."

Boosting the jurors onto their shoulders, the players carried them around the courtroom. Cicotte and Risberg rushed out right afterwards to a telegraph office where they notified their wives of the decision.

The jurors and players went off to a local Italian restaurant. There the celebration started up all over again and did not end until the wee small hours of the morning.

The next day the banner headline in the *Chicago Daily Tribune,* which sold for two cents and billed itself as the world's greatest paper, declared: JURY FREES BASEBALL MEN. The headline that led off the main story on page one said: ALL BLACKSOX ACQUITTED ON SINGLE BALLOT.

WHITE SOX PLAYERS ARE NOT GUILTY was the banner headline in the *Buffalo Express.*

CHARGES OF CONSPIRACY DO NOT HOLD was the subhead.

The Associated Press reported that the news was greeted with "surprise, disappointment and chagrin" by sports editors and writers, and added that the trial's outcome was a "travesty" and as "stunning and disturbing as the original disclosures."

Henry Ford's *Dearborn Independent* unleashed anti-Semitic propaganda in response to the verdict. Jews were in the majority behind the scenes in the bribing of players in all affairs dealing with the 1919 World Series, it stated. Ford's personal house organ excoriated Jews for soiling the good name of American sports, particularly baseball. But *The Sporting News* had one of its finest moments in its attack on the *Dearborn Independent*'s point of view. It clearly exposed the publication's outright bigotry.

The *New York World* printed the most ominous reaction to the verdict, foreshadowing what lay ahead: "If the crooks who were acquitted show their faces in decent sporting circles, they should be boycotted and blackballed."

The euphoria of the players and Comiskey at the turn of events, and their time of celebration was all too brief. Kenesaw Mountain Landis would blow out their candles, banishing them from baseball for life. Seven players acquitted by a court of law plus Fred McMullin, who was not even under indictment, were never to play professional ball again. Nor would Joe Gedeon of the St. Louis Browns, who would be added to the Landis list several months later for "having guilty knowledge."

It took only one day after the verdict was announced for Commissioner Kenesaw Mountain Landis to issue his terse statement:

"Regardless of the verdicts of juries, no player who entertains proposals or promises to throw a game, no player who sits in conference with a bunch of crooked players and gamblers where the ways and means of throwing games are discussed and does not promptly tell the club about it will ever play professional baseball."

9

First Man Out

When Judge Kenesaw Mountain Landis banished Joe Jackson and the others from organized baseball despite their being found not guilty in a court of law, it was a crossroads time for America and for baseball. The Black Sox Scandal, the banning for life of the "eight men out," the introduction of a Commissioner with dictatorial powers to "clean up the game," even the lively ball and the power of the home run bat—all were markers of a turning point in American history. An innocence was lost, never to be regained. A statement seemed appropriate, even imperative, that the easygoing, often shady ways of the past would no longer be tolerated. The Sox were the medium for that statement.

The future was beckoning. That summer, KDKA in Pittsburgh beamed the first radio broadcast of a major league baseball game. Harold Arlin described the action as the Pirates defeated the Phillies 8–5. Grantland Rice announced the World Series that year when the Yankees and Giants played at the Polo Grounds. More than 3 million Americans had at least one radio by then.

Shoeless Joe was then thirty-three years old. He was at the point in his career—especially with offensive production booming—where even greater on-the-field accomplishments seemed there for the doing. But the doing would never be done. Jackson and the others were cut off in their prime from the game they loved and the livelihood they depended on.

They were the scapegoats—eight players born in the candlelit time of the nineteenth century struck by lightning in the twentieth century.

WESTBROOK PEGLER: "You cannot fire someone because he does not put forth his best efforts for his employer. In this case the employer fired the boys and conspired with all the other employers in the same line of business to keep them out of the business forever."

Banned from organized baseball, Shoeless Joe and the other Black Sox players became easy marks for hustlers. They played pickup games whenever and wherever they could. Relentless, Judge Landis exerted his influence through the length and breadth of organized baseball to see that there would be no competition against what he called in private the "unholy eight."

JUDGE LANDIS: "They can't come back. The doors are closed to them for good. The most scandalous chapter in the game's history is closed for good on the Black Sox participants."

Joe Jackson persisted, drifting down to the shadows, playing in the Million Dollar League in Waycross, Americus, and Savannah, Georgia, in Okeechobee, Florida. Insisting that he was innocent, a victim of a vendetta, he resorted to aliases and disguises. He was a pariah, towering even above his legend, playing out the game he loved, playing out his life.

There was a game on June 22, 1922, at the Oval in Hackensack, New Jersey, against Bogota. In center field for the team from Jersey was a tall and muscular newcomer, a left-handed batter playing under the name of Joseph. He came to bat and drew a line three inches out from the plate from front to back and a right-angle line at the end next to the catcher. He put his left foot on the imaginary line exactly three inches from the plate. He kept both feet together and took a long and graceful stride into the pitched ball. A double in his first at bat. A single in his second. Then he hammered the ball out of the park for a home run. The fans were agog at a throw he cut loose that nailed a runner at home attempting to score from second base.

Hackensack won the game, but its victory was short-lived. The game was declared a forfeit when it was discovered that Joseph was Shoeless Joe Jackson, come North to pick up a payday.

Two days later, Joe Jackson and the "Ex-Major Leaguers" played a game in Merrill, Wisconsin. Swede Risberg was the manager of the team. Still the hard guy, Risberg knocked out two of Eddie Cicotte's teeth in a hotel room brawl over money.

The Savannah Valet Business occupied Joe and Katie Jackson and kept them solvent through the winters in Georgia, but baseball was something he could not and did not want to get out of his system. There was the stint along with Swede Risberg and Eddie Cicotte in Louisiana in what the press called "an outlaw league." The trio played for the Bastrop team, providing the pitching and the power to totally dominate the circuit. In thirty-five games Jackson, now playing under the name Johnson, batted above .500 and slugged long home runs. His talent once again gave him away, and his time in Louisiana came to an abrupt end.

On April 10, 1923, newspapers reported that Joe Jackson had filed a $119, 000 lawsuit against Charles Comiskey for alleged breach of contract. The figure was for the amount due on Jackson's White Sox contract, which had two years to run, plus $100,000 for slander, and $1,500 claimed to be the amount due him as his share from the 1919 World Series. Attorney George M. Hudnall, employed by Alfred Austrian, said Jackson admitted receiving $5,000 from gamblers and that his wife corroborated this. Hudnall also pulled a rabbit out of a hat: Jackson's confession, missing since 1920.

The jury in Milwaukee ruled in Jackson's favor, deciding he was owed $16,711.04. However, Judge John J. Gregory reversed the decision on the basis of contradictions: Jackson's confession in 1920 and his subsequent denial of the confession and claim of innocence. Ruling that Jackson had committed perjury, the judge ordered him jailed for a couple of days.

Upon his release, a frustrated Jackson vowed never to have anything to do with baseball again. "God knows I did my best in baseball at all times," he said, "and no man on earth can truthfully judge otherwise."

From Milwaukee it was announced that Jackson's attorneys planned to appeal. It never happened.

JOE JACKSON: "Judge Landis promised me I'd be reinstated if I was cleared by the civil court. The court threw out the case, but I was never reinstated. Baseball hasn't kept faith with me. I don't intend to ask any favors of it."

In 1926, six years after the Black Sox scandal took place, Tiger pitcher Dutch Leonard claimed he had letters from Joe Wood, Tris Speaker, and Ty Cobb concerning their bets on a game played on September 25, 1919. Rushing to the defense of these legends, baseball columnists said such charges were unbelievable.

JOE JACKSON: "Judge Landis ordered me to testify when they were investigating Cobb and Tris Speaker. I asked my lawyer about it, and he said I didn't have to go. It was none of my business. I owed nothing to baseball. I had given them my word once and they wouldn't take it. I didn't go."

Leonard also didn't go. Cobb and Speaker wanted Leonard to attend a meeting in the office of the commissioner, but he refused, stating, "I have had my revenge."

"The American League, in a secret meeting, decided they were guilty," according to sportswriter Fred Lieb, "and would let them slip out of baseball quietly, without humiliation." Speaker agreed to retire, but Cobb did not. He proclaimed his innocence, threatened to sue baseball, and make known all of its corruption. Landis bypassed the American League decision. Both Cobb and Speaker stayed in the game as players. Cobb pulled back his threats.

FRED LIEB: "I have no question about their guilt. To me the evidence was damnable."

In 1929, Joe and Katie moved from Savannah back to Greenville. Jackson occupied himself with his various business interests and whenever possible went out to watch the Greenville Sally League club play.

JOE JACKSON: "The people in my own community have

stood by me. They have never doubted me. That's why I came
back to Brandon Mills when I started looking for a place to
'light.' I'll always love the place and the people here."

Charles Comiskey died at the age of seventy-one in 1931.
A year later a *New York Sun* article provided a retrospective on
the "Black Sox" players:

> Cicotte—knuckle ball, Lefty Williams with sweeping curve,
> Risberg, a dazzling shortstop, Happy Felsch, a fielding fool,
> Buck Weaver, the best third baseman in the game and Chick
> Gandil, the slick first baseman—all scattered—a couple to
> the midwest, the rest to the far west—only Jackson still
> playing with his black bat, clear-eyed, ruddy-faced, big-
> bellied, slow moving, soft spoken, is a businessman by winter
> and a ballplayer in the summer. The 44-year-old Jackson
> weighs 220 pounds and could pass for a cotton planter or the
> owner of a cotton plantation. Runs Savannah Valet Service,
> a dry cleaning establishment, has two delivery trucks, two
> passenger cars, a bulldog, and lives with his wife of 24 years
> and his mother who is paralyzed. A huge picture of the 1919
> White Sox hangs over the counter in the main office.
>
> A home run on a sand lot before a small bunch of South
> Carolina farmers gives him as much of a thrill as a wallop over
> the roof of a big league stadium. A right fielder on the
> Greenville Spinners and the hitting marvel of the Carolinas.
> His new fame has spread through the Piedmont plateau and
> over the coastal plain.

JOE JACKSON: "I make more money pressing pants than I
ever made in the big leagues. I could lead either of the big
leagues in hitting even today. A couple of years ago playing
down here at Waycross, I hit .535 in 100 games. In the majors
for my career I hit nearly .400, didn't I? I had the record for
most hits in a series until Pepper Martin tied it, didn't I? I threw
out men at the plate and led both teams at the bat in the 1919
Series. If you ask me, I got the dirtiest deal any man in organized baseball ever got. I ain't ever asked Judge Landis for re-

instatement. I don't suppose he'd give it to me if I did. But I
believe I could get back in there right now. I'd like to have a
couple of months to get back in real shape and then if I figured
I was all right I'd go to it. And if I couldn't lead my club in hitting, I'd work without pay. Why, there's a couple of boys down
here who are pitching as good as anything I ever saw up in the
big league.

"Take that Lefty Brown. He's ready right now. An' we got
a shortstop named Frazier Heath who's as good as Wagner ever
was. It's fast time down here, I'm tellin' you."

In 1932, when he was forty-three years old, Jackson applied to Landis for permission to manage a team in Greenville,
South Carolina. But the old animosity prevailed.

JUDGE LANDIS: "There are not and cannot be two stan-
dards of eligibility, one for major leagues and another (and
lower one) for minors . . . . This application must be denied. . . .
several other principles (sic) in the World Series scandal of
1919 have tried unsuccessfully to be reinstated."

One of the "principles" was Buck Weaver, who appealed
six times to Landis for reinstatement; each time he was turned
down. One time a petition asking for his pardon signed by
14,000 Chicago and northern Illinois Masons was brought to
the office of the Baseball Commissioner.

JUDGE LANDIS: "I had Weaver in this office. I asked him
'Buck, did you ever sit in on any meeting to throw the 1919
World Series?' He replied, 'Yes, Judge, I attended two such
meetings, but I took no money and played the best ball I am capable of.'

"So I told him anyone who sat in on such a meeting and did
not report it was as guilty as any of the others. 'Buck, you can't
play ball with us again.' That, too, is my answer to you gentlemen."

A disconsolate Weaver had but one positive moment in all
the years of battling and appealing. Victory in a court suit provided him with a partial payment of his 1920 contract.

Kid Gleason died in 1933, at the age of sixty-seven. The
1919 White Sox had been like a bone stuck in his craw all those

years. He had never gotten over it. That year Joe Jackson was signed by the Eufaula Club of the Dixie Amateur League. But W.A. West, president of the Birmingham Club of the Southern Association, protested, claiming the signing endangered the future status of every other player in the league. With the doors barred to him there, Jackson turned to semipro baseball; he enjoyed success as a player-manager in South Georgia with the Waycross team.

JOE JACKSON: "I can still hit as good as I ever did and I'm tellin' you down here there's some of the toughest pitchin' you ever saw. I've been averaging two hits a game, and generally am good for at least a home run a game. A fly ball looks just like it used to look—just as easy to catch. At running I'm not so good. When I have to run I can do it, I guess. But I just sort of trot out my singles and doubles and walk out my home runs."

At the age of forty-six, Joe Jackson took up his famous stance for the last time in Winnsboro, South Carolina, as manager of a semipro team. Then he turned his fulltime attention to the retail liquor store he owned in Greenville while also serving as a member of the protest board of the Western Carolina League, a textile organization. In 1937, at age fifty and weighing 230 pounds—55 pounds more than when he played—Jackson mused about this life.

JOE JACKSON: "I got two autos and money in the bank. The thing I like to think of most is my World Series record of 1919—the one I got put out of baseball for. I made twelve hits in that series and nobody—not even the Babe—ever did that until Pepper Martin came along a few years ago. Twelve hits—and they throw me out of baseball. . . . Sure I'd love to be in the game, love to have something, anything to do with it. But I'd rather be out than be in and bossed by a czar. I'd sort of like to be playing these days 'cause I think with the live ball, I could give 'em a run for their money. I haven't been to a major league game since 1932 when I dropped into Yankee Stadium one day when I was visiting New York City. Wish I coulda stepped up to the plate that day. I just know I coulda banged one out of the lot. My eyes are as good as ever."

On his fifty-fourth birthday in 1942 a huge crowd came out in the rain to attend Joe Jackson Appreciation Night staged at Brandon Field near the spot where he played his first baseball. The field was changed; home plate was now where center field was when he had played, and a concrete grandstand occupied the area where the dump in center field used to be.

When Jackson arrived, the people started yelling: "You got a raw deal, Joe, you got a tough break . . . You belong in the Hall of Fame!"

There were a few speeches. Then gifts were presented. One of them was a floral horseshoe from the Greenville Sally League team. "Greenville, Greenville," he said, recalling his first professional baseball experience. "Greenville in the Carolina League."

Then the hat was passed around just as his younger brothers had done those years gone by. Fans reached into their pockets and purses and dropped in coins. Joe did not need or want the money but he took it, an echo of time gone by.

JOE JACKSON: "I never pulled away from the plate as long as I was in baseball. And that goes from the time I played on the sandlots through my professional career and to the end of my active days as a volunteer manager of the Woodside-Mills semi-pro team in 1937. No sir, I never pulled away. I gave the game all I had, and I'm now willing to share all I've got to make some poor soul smile.

"I had no experience with the so-called rabbit ball, and how are we to judge whether the current ball is livelier? Maybe there are more good hitters on each club now than in my time. This would account for a higher club batting average in contrast to the old .250 team averages when a few of us managed to hit around .400. I imagine they've got great players as we had in our day, but I really would like to see Lajoie, Honus Wagner, Tris Speaker, and Cobb hitting up there today in their prime."

That same year of 1942, Jackson gave a long interview to *The Sporting News*. "Regardless of what anybody says, I was innocent of any wrongdoing. I gave baseball all I had. The Supreme Being is the only one to whom I've got to answer. If I had been out there booting balls and looking foolish at bat against the Reds, there might have been some grounds for suspicion. I think my record in the 1919 World Series will stand up against that of any man in that Series or any World Series in history."

Judge Landis died in November of 1944. A month later he was enshrined in the National Baseball Hall of Fame. Two years later, Hugh Fullerton passed away at age seventy-two. The old adversaries were departing. The old demons, too, had more or less been exorcised from Joe Jackson's psyche.

On April 21, 1945, Ty Cobb selected his all-time All Star team: George Sisler, first base; Eddie Collins, second base; Honus Wagner, shortstop; Buck Weaver, third base; Joe Jackson, left field; Tris Speaker, center field; Babe Ruth, right field; and pitchers Ed Walsh, Walter Johnson, Grover Cleveland Alexander, Christy Mathewson, and Ed Plank.

"I have placed Weaver and Jackson," said Cobb, "[but] am only judging them on their ability."

Jackson's all-time American League All Star team was similar to Cobb's: George Sisler, first base; Eddie Collins, second base; Buck Weaver, third base; Ray Chapman, shortstop; Cobb, Speaker, and Ruth, outfield; Steve O'Neil, catcher; and pitchers Walter Johnson, Harry Krause, Joe Wood, Ed Walsh, and Vean Gregg and Connie Mack was his pick as manager.

Ty Cobb, Babe Ruth, and Tris Speaker all named Joe Jackson the greatest natural hitter of all time. Ted Williams later sought out many of those who played with and against Jackson, questioning them on his style.

TED WILLIAMS: "I wanted to hit like Jackson. Ty Cobb told me, 'There was the greatest, son, and there's been nothing like him, since or before.'

"I have one regret about the time I played. Year after year when we headed north after spring training I never stopped off in Greenville to visit Joe Jackson."

As the 1940s came to an end, Joe Jackson was a familiar sight driving around Greenville in his Packard that seemed to always need oil. He wore white shirts and silk neckties and

lived comfortably at 119 East Wilburn Street in a brick bunga-
low surrounded by a white picket fence. It was a quiet little
street in a secluded, moderate-income neighborhood on the
south side of Greenville. From the back porch he could see the
sprawl of Brandon Mills, where he had played his first game of
baseball.

But time and tragedy had taken their toll. A liver condition
gradually cut his weight from 240 to 150. A heart condition
racked his once powerful body. He became even more interested in teaching young boys how to play baseball.

JOE JACKSON: "I can't play any more on account of my
heart, but I can watch ball games the rest of my life."

In 1951, the South Carolina House of Representatives
passed the first of several resolutions urging Jackson's reinstatement. The resolution was introduced by Representatives John
J. Snow of Williamsburg and Frank Eppes of Greenville.

"Fact and fancy have been so confused," the resolution
noted, "that today it is still not known what actually took place
(in the Series). . . . Thirty-two years is too long for any man to
be penalized for an act . . . (when there was) strong evidence
that he was no party to the conspiracy." The resolution stated
it was unfair that the ex-star should suffer "life long ignominy"
as a result of the scandal.

When Jackson heard about the resolution, he commented:
"I greatly appreciate what all the boys did for me. I thank them
from the bottom of my heart."

Sportswriter Furman Bisher's commentary in the *Atlanta
Constitution* supported the resolution and the movement to
clear Jackson's name. "I spent a few days with Jackson in his
mill village home near Greenville. . . . He was a man who had
been brought up to know sin when he saw it, and this was sin
in capital letters. Jackson said to me, 'I'm not what you call a
Christian, but I believe in the good book. What you sow, so
shall you reap. I asked the Lord for guidance, and I'm sure he
gave it to me. No man who has done the things they accuse me
of could have been so successful.'

"The greatest event that could happen in the life of Joe Jackson, a man who has known the height of success and the bitter depths of despairing disappointment, would be complete exoneration by baseball. It would add years to his life and bring a smile to a face calloused by bitterness."

Both Bisher's commentary and the South Carolina resolution were ignored by Commissioner Happy Chandler.

Although the National Baseball Hall of Fame in Cooperstown was off limits to Jackson, the Cleveland Baseball Hall of Fame elected him to its ranks along with Tris Speaker, Earl Averill, Mel Harder, and others. To commemorate the event, Jackson was scheduled for a December 16, 1951, appearance on Ed Sullivan's "Toast of the Town." A presentation of a lifetime gold clock was to be made by Tris Speaker and sportswriter Ed Bang. Since Jackson was in poor health, having suffered three heart attacks in the previous couple of years, arrangements were made for him to travel with Katie, a physician, and "Scoop" Latimer, veteran sports editor of the *Greenville News*.

A week before the planned trip to New York for the Ed Sullivan Show, Jackson was working at his liquor store in West Greenville when he complained that he felt sick. He was taken home, and he went to bed early. The next morning at about 9:30, he awoke with a severe pain in his chest. His wife Katie and his brother David were with him. Jackson gripped his brother's hand.

JOE JACKSON: "The good Lord will know I'm innocent. Goodbye, good buddy. This is it."

At 10:15 Joseph Jefferson Jackson suffered a massive heart attack and died before the doctor arrived. The death certificate noted his age as sixty-three years.

The funeral took place in Brandon Baptist Church in Greenville as Jackson had wished. The rites were simple and spare. The survivors present included his wife, two sisters, and five brothers. Hundreds of former mill workers, men who had played with him on baseball teams and semipro clubs, and a few former major leaguers came to pay their last respects. So many flowers were brought to the cemetery that there was no place to put them. They were simply heaped in a huge mound over his grave. Among the condolences sent to the family were those from Charles Albert Comiskey, the grandson of the Old Roman.

When Ty Cobb heard the news in Menlo Park, California, he said, "He was a good man and a great ballplayer."

Joseph Jefferson Jackson left behind a dozen scrapbooks, most of them filled with faded newspaper clippings:

WARHOP GROOVES 3–0 ON JACKSON

SHOELESS JOE SLAMS HOMER TO WIN GAME FOR SOX IN TENTH 1–0

THE PRIDE OF CLEVELAND HAS A GLOVE WHERE TRIPLES GO TO DIE

Other headlines spoke of his managing to record a hit the first time up with every club he ever played for, his record—the longest home run ever measured at the Polo Grounds—and the 500-foot home run he hit at Waycross, Georgia.

There were batches of letters sent to him through the years from all over the country. Most were handwritten, yellowed, and wrinkled.

There was a laminated plaque with this statement from Jackson: "Baseball gave me my greatest thrill when I was up there hitting, running, fielding, throwing. I hardly know which was my biggest single thrill."

And there was Black Betsy on a shelf in the garage, its handle crooked with age.

Joe Jackson was the first man out.

Fred McMullin died in Los Angeles in 1952 at age sixty-one.

Buck Weaver, who never joined the others in outlaw semi-pro games, drifted from job to job. His last one was as a parimutuel clerk. He died of a heart attack in Chicago in 1956 at the age of sixty-six.

Lefty Williams ran a poolroom in Chicago for a time, just getting by. Later he became a manager of a landscaping business in Laguna Beach, California, where he died at age sixty-six in November of 1959.

Happy Felsch ran a tavern in Milwaukee and was constantly embroiled in fights with argumentative drinkers about 1919.

Felsch finally got tired of arguing and gave it up. He died at the age of seventy-three in 1964.

Eddie Cicotte lived under an assumed name most of the time and moved from job to job: game warden, security guard, near the end sweeping off snow from driveways in the winter and raising strawberries in the summers. In 1969, he died at age eighty-five in Detroit.

Chick Gandil was a plumber and a tinkerer at odd jobs. The last part of his life was spent in the beautiful Napa Valley of Northern California. In 1970, in the aptly named town of St. Helena, his time ran out. He was eighty-two.

Swede Risberg spent many years as a dairy farmer in Minnesota. Then he moved on to California. It was there that he passed away at the age of eighty-one in 1975, the last man out.

10

Afterwards

God knows I gave my best in baseball at all times and no man on earth can truthfully judge me otherwise.
—JOE JACKSON

It is nearly seventy-five years since the "Black Sox" scandal, yet the controversy particularly as it relates to Joe Jackson persists. If anything, interest in the subject has increased, along with efforts to urge the power structure to open the gates of the Baseball Hall of Fame to Shoeless Joe.

FURMAN BISHER: "Look into a case that wreaks with injustice. Though all that's left is a headstone in a cemetery and a name vague in a lot of memories, there's a debt that can only be paid off in Cooperstown."

In 1989, the senate in Jackson's home state of South Carolina passed a unanimous resolution asking organized baseball to exonerate him with the hope that he would one day be able to be admitted to the National Baseball Hall of Fame. But Baseball Commissioner A. Bartlett Giamatti turned down the request.

A. BARTLETT GIAMATTI: "For good reason there has not been a reconsideration. . . . The events around the 1919 World Series and its aftermath cannot be recreated, in my opinion, in sufficient detail and depth to provide a firm enough basis to take an action today that would change Mr. Jackson's place in history.

185

"I for one do not wish to play God with history. The Jackson case is now best left to historical analysis and debate as opposed to a present-day review with an eye to reinstatement."

Giamatti, the commissioner who expelled Pete Rose from baseball, simply sidestepped the issue of Joe Jackson.

Today, there are photographs of Joe Jackson on the walls of the Hall of Fame at Cooperstown; a pair of his shoes rest in a glass case there. But Joseph Jefferson Jackson is still the odd man out, while year after year other players with far less extraordinary records are admitted.

Through all the years he consistently denied any wrongdoing. The Grand Jury testimony—which appears as an appendix in this book, published in full for the first time anywhere—states for the record that he played his best to win in that 1919 World Series. And indeed, anyone looking at the record sees that he fielded flawlessly, had the most hits, the highest batting average, the only home run.

So many questions remain unanswered. How does one square the inconsistencies between newspaper accounts of Jackson's testimony and his actual testimony? How much stock should be placed in the confession, signed with an "X", of a man who could neither read nor write? Was the confession obtained under false pretenses, coaxed out of Jackson by Austrian with promises he could go anywhere in the world he wanted and be free from worry about going to jail if only he confessed to the Grand Jury? Innocent men have confessed to far more serious crimes when promised far less.

If there was a plan to throw the Series, was it carried out? It so, which games were thrown? Which plays were deliberate misplays, which were natural errors? Years later, Chick Gandil commented that he felt the banning was unjust, "but I truthfully never resented it because even though the Series wasn't thrown, we were guilty of a serious offense and we knew it." If the Series was not thrown, what was the serious offense?

How much money did each White Sox player receive? And for what? Buck Weaver apparently received none. Jackson's share of $5,000 was purportedly dumped into his room, and he ran around with it encased in a dirty envelope trying to convince anyone in power to take it. No one, not even Bill Burns, placed Jackson at any of the meetings of the gamblers. About the only charge substantiated against Jackson is that he had "guilty knowledge" of what was taking place. Yet he maintained that when he attempted to tell Comiskey of what was happening, he was rebuffed.

Was Charles Comiskey guilty of a cover-up? If knowledge was tantamount to guilt, as Landis told Buck Weaver in denying him the right to play the game, why did Grabiner and Comiskey escape Landis's judgment? Comiskey claimed his investigation led to confessions that ultimately cost him the pennant and hundreds of thousands of dollars. But the facts suggest that Comiskey acted only when the Maharg story hit the front pages all over the country.

Once the trial was on, did Comiskey attempt to save his team from destruction by supplying favorable witnesses? Did he pay the bill for all the high-powered legal talent who represented the accused?

What can be said of the behavior of Alfred Austrian, who made Jackson believe he was acting on his behalf when the lawyer was actually preparing a scapegoat who would tell a story Comiskey and Grabiner wanted told? Shouldn't each defendant have had his own lawyer from the start? How can a lawyer encourage his client to waive immunity, thereby paving the way for his confession to be used against him in a criminal trial?

Was due process served? It was obvious that there were different levels of guilt. Why the blanket indictment, the blanket sentence from Landis? Why were the eight White Sox the only ones to be penalized? Why was no gambler ever brought to justice?

In a 1984 article in *The Boston Herald,* attorney Alan Dershowitz suggests such unevenly applied justice would not be tolerated today. "An honest prosecutor generally seeks to follow the criminal trail to the top of the mountain," writes Dershowitz. "Convicting the Watergate burglars was not enough.

The special prosecutor followed the trail to the attorney general and eventually to the president.

"But in post World War I Chicago, corruption tainted more than the White Sox," he adds. "The entire city—judiciary and all—reeked with influence-peddling and power brokering, and among the most influential brokers was Charles Comiskey."

Perhaps it is all of the unanswered questions as well as a powerful sense that justice miscarried, that the ignorant were duped by the clever, that the powerless suffered and the strong prevailed, that makes the story of Shoeless Joe Jackson and his teammates live on.

There is no end to the public's fascination with the illiterate South Carolina baseball player banned from the game he loved for a crime he may not have committed. Today, a decent-quality 1914 Cracker Jack baseball card portraying Joe Jackson is worth about $5,000. In 1990, at an auction in New York City, a scrap of paper bearing the shaky signature of Joe Jackson sold for $23,100, the top sum paid for any nineteenth- or twentieth-century autograph and the second-highest ever paid at auction for an unattached signature. (The record of $56,000 was paid for the rare signature of Button Gwinnett, a signer of the Declaration of Independence.) Jackson's signature was found on a shred of paper just 4-by-1½ inches, cut out from a building transaction document that he signed in April 1936. The value undoubtedly stems from its rarity: only about a half-dozen authentic Joe Jackson signatures are known to exist. Only a few legal documents bear his hand, including his White Sox contracts of 1919 and 1920. While many "signed" Joe Jackson baseballs surfaced in the years he had the liquor store in Greenville, these were all neatly autographed by Katie. Such a to-do over the scrawlings of a man who could not write. It's like the Cole Porter song: "The world's gone mad today, and good's bad today, and black's white today, and day's night today. . . ."

Shoeless Joe Jackson never won a batting title. But four times in his career he batted over .370. His batting average for the 1910s was .354, and his slugging average was over .500. His lifetime batting average of .356 is the third-highest of all those who have ever played the game. Only Cobb at .367 and Rogers Hornsby at .357 recorded higher marks. Jackson is the only player ever to hit over .400 and not win a batting title.

They tried to exorcise his spirit from the game. But his black bat, blue darters, and slashing swings have stitched him into the tapestry of the national pastime nevertheless. Although cast out from the game he loved, he never became an outcast. His fall from grace never neutered his persona; it only served to enhance the myth. Often maligned and misunderstood during his lifetime, he has become a folk hero after death, the representative of a collective nostalgic yearning for an agrarian past.

He is forever the image of the poor barefoot boy playing baseball in the cow pastures who high-steps it all the way to the top of the hill in the major leagues. He has become an American icon alongside Daniel Webster, Paul Bunyan, Johnny Appleseed, Davey Crockett, Billy the Kid, and Jesse James, hero and at the same time antihero. As a mythic character, he appears in our stories and songs. He is the Faustian fantasy of eternal youth in the musical show *Damn Yankees*—"Shoeless Joe from Hannibal Mo." He is the inspiration behind Bernard Malamud's hero in his novel *The Natural*. He is the central presence of W.P. Kinsella's *Shoeless Joe*.

The movie *Field of Dreams,* based on Kinsella's book, completes the mythology. There is a scene in the film in which a young Joe Jackson emerges from a man-high field of corn. In his youthful handsomeness is the proof of his immortality. Politely, but with intense seriousness, darkly quiet, he proceeds in a kind of religious ritual to call out of the cornstalks his fellow players of a time long gone by. One by one, they assemble on the cleared field under his direction and take their places. Then silently, in the dusk, they begin the slow pantomime of their game.

It is no more than a movie. Yet since its release an odd thing has happened. Thousands of people, from all over the country, have come to visit this Iowa cornfield. For some reason, they have taken literally the message of the film: "They will come."

It has become an American mecca of sorts and the journey to this place a modern-day pilgrimage. It is only a cleared field in the heartland of the country, surrounded by acres and acres of towering corn. Yet it is a common destination for throngs of visitors who look at the open expanse and conjure up the image of the one-time South Carolina millboy who, playing in his bare feet, could hit and run and catch and field like no one else—Shoeless Joe Jackson.

Appendix

The Grand Jury Testimony of Joe Jackson

(as recorded by E.A. Eulass & Co., Court and
General Stenographic Reporters)

BASEBALL INQUIRY   Tuesday, September 28, 1920
GRAND JURY   3:00 P.M.

JOE JACKSON,

called as a witness, having been first duly sworn, testified as
follows:

EXAMINATION BY
Mr. Replogle

Q Mr. Jackson, you understand that any testimony you may
give here can be used in evidence against you at any future trial;
you know who I am, I am State's Attorney, and this is the Grand
Jury, this is the Foreman of the Grand Jury. Now, I will read this
immunity waiver to you so you will know just what it is:

"Chicago, Illinois, September 28, 1920. I, Joe Jackson, the
undersigned, of my own free will make this my voluntary statement and am willing to testify and do testify before the Grand
Jury with full knowledge of all the facts and of my legal rights,
knowing full well that any testimony I may give might incrim-
inate me, and might be used against me in any case of prosecution or connected with the subject matter of my testimony, and
now having been fully advised as to my legal rights, I hereby

191

with said full knowledge waive all immunity that I might claim by reason of my appearing before the Grand Jury and giving testimony concerning certain crimes of which I have knowledge."

(Whereupon the witness signed the foregoing document)

Q What is your name?
A Joe. Jackson.

Q Where do you live, Mr. Jackson?
A You mean in the City here?

Q Where is your home?
A Greenville, South Carolina.

Q What is your business?
A Baseball player.

Q How long have you been playing professional baseball?
A Since 1908.

Q Where have you played professional baseball?
A Why, I started out in Greenville, South Carolina; went from there to Philadelphia, Philadelphia Americans.

Q How long were you with them?
A I went in the fall of 1908, and went to Savannah, Georgia.

Q How long were you there?
A Finished the season there, and I was called back by the Athletics; from there went to New Orleans, in 1910; 1910 in the fall I came to Cleveland and stayed with Cleveland until 1915, and I have been here ever since.

Q Did you play with the White Sox from 1915?
A About the middle of the season I was there.

Q Are you married or single?
A Married.

Q How long have you been married?
A Been married thirteen years this coming July.

Q Have you any children?
A No, sir.

Q Is your wife in Chicago at the present time?

A Yes, sir.

Q Where is your Chicago address?

A Trenier Hotel, 40th and Grand Boulevard.

Q You were playing professional ball with the White Sox in the season of 1919, were you?

A Yes, sir.

Q You played in the World Series between the Chicago Americans Baseball Club and the Cincinnati Baseball Club, did you?

A I did.

Q What position did you play in that series?

A Left Field.

Q Were you present at a meeting at the Ansonia Hotel in New York about two or three weeks before—a conference there with a number of ball players?

A I was not, no, sir.

Q Did anybody pay you any money to help throw that series in favor of Cincinnati?

A They did.

Q How much did they pay?

A They promised me $20,000, and paid me five.

Q Who promised you the twenty thousand?

A "Chick" Gandil.

Q Who is Chick Gandil?

A He was their first baseman on the White Sox Club.

Q Who paid you the $5,000?

A Lefty Williams brought it in my room and threw it down.

Q Who is Lefty Williams?

A The pitcher on the White Sox Club.

Q Where did he bring it, where is your room?

A At that time I was staying at the Lexington Hotel, I believe it is.

Q On 21st and Michigan?

A 22nd and Michigan, yes.

Q Who was in the room at the time?
A Lefty and myself, I was in there, and he came in.

Q Where was Mrs. Jackson?
A Mrs. Jackson—let me see—I think she was in the bathroom. It was a suite; yes, she was in the bathroom, I am pretty sure.

Q Does she know that you got $5,000 for helping throw these games?
A She did that night, yes.

Q You say you told Mrs. Jackson that evening?
A Did, yes.

Q What did she say about it?
A She said she thought it was an awful thing to do.

Q When was it that this money was brought to your room and that you talked to Mrs. Jackson?
A It was the second trip to Cincinnati. That night we were leaving.

Q That was after the fourth game?
A I believe it was, yes.

Q Refreshing your recollection, the first two games that you remember were played in Cincinnati?
A Yes, sir.

Q And the second two were played here?
A Yes.

Q This was after the four games?
A Yes, sir.

Q You were going back to Cincinnati?
A Yes, sir.

Q What time of the day was it that he came to your rooms?
A It was between, I would say, 7 and 8 o'clock in the evening, right after the game.

Q After the fourth game? Do you remember who won that game?
A Dick Kerr, I believe.

Q Cincinnati won that game, Cicotte pitched and Cincinnati won; do you remember now? Cincinnati beat you 2 to nothing?
A Yes, sir.

Q Were you at a conference of these men, these players on the Sox team, at the Warner Hotel sometime previous to this?
A No, sir, I was not present, but I knew they had the meeting, so I was told.

Q Who told you?
A Williams.

Q Who else talked to you about this besides Claude Williams?
A Claude didn't talk to me direct about it, he just told me things that had been said.

Q What did he tell you?
A He told me about this meeting in particular, he said the gang was there, and this fellow Attel, Abe Attel, I believe, and Bill Burns is the man that give him the double crossing, as Gandil told me.

Q You say Abe Attel and Bill Burns are the two people that Claude Williams told you gave you the double cross?
A Chick Gandil told me that.

Q Then you talked to Chick Gandil and Claude Williams both about this?
A Talked to Claude Williams about it, yes, and Gandil more so, because he is the man that promised me this stuff.

Q How much did he promise you?
A $20,000 if I would take part.

Q And you said you would?
A Yes, sir.

Q When did he promise you the $20,000?
A It was to be paid after each game.

Q How much?
A Split it up some way, I don't know just how much it amounts to, but during the series it would amount to $20,000. Finally Williams brought me this $5,000, threw it down.

Q What did you say to Williams when he threw down the $5,000?

A I asked him what the hell had come off here.

Q What did he say?

A He said Gandil said we all got a screw through Abe Attel. Gandil said that we got double crossed through Abe Attel, he got the money and refused to turn it over to him. I don't think Gandil was crossed as much as he crossed us.

Q You think Gandil may have gotten the money and held it from you, is that right?

A That's what I think, I think he kept the majority of it.

Q What did you do then?

A I went to him and asked him what was the matter. He said Abe Attel gave him the jazzing. He said, "Take that or let it alone." As quick as the series was over I left town, I went right on out.

Q Did you ever meet Abe Attel?

A Not to my knowledge, no sir. I wouldn't know him if I would see him.

Q Did you ever meet Bill Burns?

A Yes, sir.

Q Where did you first meet Bill Burns?

A When I first came in the American League to play ball I first met him.

Q Where was he then?

A He was at Detroit when I met him.

Q Do you know whether or not he was in on this deal?

A Well, I know what Gandil told me, that he and Attel was the men that—

Q Bill Burns and Abe Attel?

A Yes.

Q Were the men that what?

A And some other gentlemen, I can't recall their names. There was three of them.

Q A Jewish name, if you know, would you know it if you were to hear it?

A No, sir, I would not.

Q Do you know whether or not Gedeon of St. Louis was in on this in any way?

A No, sir, I only know he was with Risberg and McMullin all the time.

Q Whom, Gedeon?

A That's all I know. I seen him around with them.

Q What is his first name?

A Joe.

Q Joe Gedeon? Do you know whether or not Rawlins of the Philadelphia National League Club was in on this in any way?

A No, sir, I do not.

Q You know Rawlins?

A I only know him by name.

Q You know Gedeon?

A Yes.

Q Where did you see McMullin and Risberg together?

A In Cincinnati one night in the smoking room of a Pullman car.

Q Where else?

A And I saw them on the street together in Cincinnati. I didn't see them in Chicago here, because I didn't live in that neighborhood, though I would see Joe at the ball grounds.

Q You saw. Gedeon?

A Yes.

Q At the ball park during the World Series?

A Yes, I saw him here one day, I saw him in here.

Q And you were to be paid $5,000 after each game, is that right?

A Well, Attel was supposed to give the $100,000. It was to be split up, paid to him, I believe, and $15,000 a day or something like that, after each game.

Q That is to Gandil?
A Yes.

Q At the end of the first game you didn't get any money, did you?
A No, I did not, no, sir.

Q What did you do then?
A I asked Gandil what is the trouble? He says, "Everything is all right," he had it.

Q Then you went ahead and threw the second game, thinking you would get it then, is that right?
A We went ahead and threw the second game, we went after him again. I said to him, "What are you going to do?" "Everything is all right," he says, "What the hell is the matter?"

Q After the third game what did you say to him?
A After the third game I says, "Somebody is getting a nice little jazz, everybody is crossed." He said, "well, Abe Attel and Bill Burns had crossed him, that is what he said to me.

Q He said Abe Attel and Bill Burns had crossed him?
A Yes, sir.

Q After the fourth game, did you talk to him then before Williams brought you the money?
A No, sir; I didn't talk to him then, no, sir. Williams and I talked.

Q Who was your best chum on the team, who did you go with in the club?
A Williams and Lind. I hardly ever pal with any of them there except those two.

Q Who did Gandil pal with mostly on the team?
A Risberg.

Q Who did McMullin pal with mostly on the team?
A I cannot recall who McMullin roomed with.

Q Who did he go with?
A You would see him and Charlie together, and Chick, quite a bit.

Q Chick Gandil and Charlie Risberg?
A All times, not only on this occasion.

Q Do you know who was the first man that the gamblers approached, that Burns and Attel approached on your team?
A Well, I don't know who the first man was.

Q Who do you think was the man they approached?
A Why, Gandil.

Q What makes you think Gandil?
A Well, he was the whole works of it, the instigator of it, the fellow that mentioned it to me. He told me that I could take it or let it go, they were going through with it.

Q Didn't you think it was the right thing for you to go and tell Comiskey about it?
A I did tell them once, "I am not going to be in it." I will just get out of that altogether.

Q Who did you tell that to?
A Chick Gandil.

Q What did he say?
A He said I was into it already and I might as well stay in. I said, "I can go to the boss and have every damn one of you pulled out of the limelight." He said it wouldn't be well for me if I did that.

Q Gandil said to you?
A Yes, sir.

Q What did you say?
A Well, I told him any time they wanted to have me knocked off, to have me knocked off.

Q What did he say?
A Just laughed.

Q When did that conversation take place, that you said any time they wanted to have you knocked off, to have you knocked off?

A   That was the fourth game, the fifth night going back to Cincinnati. I met Chick Gandil and his wife going to the 12th Street Station. They got out of the cab there. I was standing on the corner.

Q   Do you recall the fourth game that Cicotte pitched?
A   Yes, sir.

Q   Did you see any fake plays made by yourself or anybody on that game, that would help throw the game?
A   Only the wildness of Cicotte.

Q   What was that?
A   Hitting the batter, that is the only thing that told me they were going through with it.

Q   Did you make any intentional errors yourself that day?
A   No, sir, not during the whole series.

Q   Did you bat to win?
A   Yes.

Q   And run the bases to win?
A   Yes, sir.

Q   And fielded the balls at the outfield to win?
A   I did.

Q   Did you ever hear anyone accusing Cicotte of crossing the signals that were given to him by Schalk.
A   No, sir, I did not.

Q   Do you know whether or not any of those signals were crossed by Cicotte?
A   No, sir, I couldn't say.

Q   But you didn't hear any of the boys talking about that, did you?
A   No.

Q   After the fourth game you went to Cincinnati and you had the $5,000, is that right?

A Yes, sir.

Q Where did you put the $5,000, did you put it in the bank or keep it on your person?

A I put it in my pocket.

Q What denominations, in silver or bills?

A In bills.

Q How big were some of the bills?

A Some hundreds, mostly fifties.

Q What did Mrs. Jackson say about it after she found it out again?

A She felt awful bad about it, cried about it a while.

Q Did it ever occur to you to tell about this before this?

A Yes, where I offered to come here last fall in the investigation, I would have told it last fall if they would have brought me in.

Q And you are telling this now, of course, of your own free will, you want to tell the truth, is that the idea, of all you know?

A Yes, sir.

Q In the second game, did you see any plays made by any of those fellows that would lead you to believe that they were trying to throw the game, that is the game that Claude Williams pitched with Cincinnati?

A There was wildness, too, that cost that game. Two walks, I think, and a triple by this fellow, two or three men out.

Q Was there any other moves that would lead you to believe they were throwing the game?

A No, sir, I didn't see any plays that I thought was throwing the game.

Q In the third game Kerr pitched there, 1 to nothing. Did you see anything there that would lead you to believe anyone was trying to throw the game?

A No, sir. I think if you would look that record up, I drove in two and hit one.

Q You made a home run, didn't you?

A That was in the last game here.

Q The fourth game Cicotte pitched again? It was played out here in Chicago and Chicago lost it 2 to nothing? Do you remember that?
A Yes, sir.

Q Did you see anything wrong about that game that would lead you to believe there was an intentional fixing?
A The only thing that I was sore about that game, the throw I made to the plate, Cicotte tried to intercept it.

Q It would have gone to the first base if he had not intercepted it?
A Yes.

Q Did you do anything to throw these games?
A No, sir.

Q Any game in the Series?
A Not a one. I didn't have an error or make no misplay.

Q Supposing the White Sox would have won this Series, the World's Series, what would you have done then with the $5,000?
A I guess I would have kept it, that was all I could do. I tried to win all the time.

Q To keep on with these games, the fifth game, did you see anything wrong with that or any of the games, did you see any plays that you would say might have been made to throw that particular game?
A Well, I only saw one play in the whole series, I don't remember what game it was in, either, it was in Cincinnati.

Q Who made it?
A Charlie Risberg.

Q What was that?
A It looked like a perfect double play. And he only gets one, gets the ball and runs over to the bag with it in place of throwing it in front of the bag.

Q After the series were all over, did you have any talk with any of these men?
A No, sir, I left the next night.

Q Where did you go?
A Savannah, Georgia.

Q Weren't you very much peeved that you only got $5,000 and you expected to get twenty?
A No, I was ashamed of myself.

Q Have you ever talked with Chick Gandil since that time?
A No, I never saw him since.

Q When was the last time you saw him and talked to him?
A It was on the following morning after the series were over, that day in Comiskey's office, waiting in there.

Q What did you say to him at that time?
A I told him there was a hell of a lot of scandal going around for what had happened. He said, "To hell with it." He was about half drunk. I went on out and left that night.

Q Was Chick Gandil in the habit of drinking?
A Yes, Chick liked his liquor.

Q Did you drink much, Mr. Jackson?
A Now and then, I don't make no regular practice of it.

Q Do you get drunk?
A No, sir.

Q Have you been drunk since you have been with the Chicago White Sox team?
A Yes, sir.

Q During the playing season?
A Yes, sir.

Q Where?
A Atlantic City.

Q You were not playing—
A Off days.

Q Did Mr. Comiskey or Mr. Gleason know you were drunk at that time?
A I don't judge they did, no, sir.

Q Who was with you when you got drunk?
A Claude Williams, John Fornier, and myself.

Q That is some years ago, he played with the Chicago team, is that right?
A I think it was '18.

Q You haven't been drunk since you played with the Chicago team?
A Not what you would call drunk, no.

Q Did you ever talk to Happy Felsch since that time, about those games?
A I believe I mentioned it to Happy the other day, too; Yes, I know I did.

Q What did you say to him?
A I told him they would have him down before the Grand Jury before long, the way things looked.

Q What did he say?
A He said, "All right."

Q What day was that, Mr. Jackson?
A I don't remember what day it was, but one day last week.

Q Were you playing ball?
A We were walking across the field, yes, sir. Just before practice, I believe, and we were taking our position for practice that day.

Q Do you know whether or not Happy Felsch received some of this money?
A I don't know that he received any more than what the boys said.

Q What did the boys say about him?
A They said each fellow got so much money.

Q Did they say how much?

A $5,000, I understand, Felsch.

Q Do you remember whether or not some of them got more than $5,000?

A No, sir, I don't.

Q You wouldn't say that any one got more than $5,000; in other words, if I was to tell you one man got $10,000, you wouldn't doubt it, would you; you don't know?

A Yes, I know the man you would refer to.

Q Do you know how much he got?

A I know what he said.

Q Do you know how much he said he got?

A $10,000.

Q Who do you think I mean, then?

A Eddie Cicotte.

Q When did Eddie Cicotte tell you he got $10,000?

A The next morning after the meeting we had in his room.

Q Did you tell him how much you got?

A I did.

Q What did you tell him?

A I told him I got five thousand.

Q What did he say?

A He said I was a God damn fool for not getting it in my hand like he did.

Q What did he mean by that?

A I don't know, that he wouldn't trust anybody, I guess.

Q What did he mean, that's what he meant by it?

A Why, he meant he would not trust them, they had to pay him before he did anything.

Q He meant then you ought to have got your money before you played, is that it?

A Yes, that's it.

Q Did you have a talk with any of the other players about how much they got?
A I understand McMullin got five and Risberg five thousand, that's the way I understand.

Q How do you understand that?
A Just by talking to different fellows.

Q To whom?
A Different fellows.

Q Did you talk to McMullin himself?
A Very little. I never talked to Mac any more than just hello and go on.

Q Did you ever ask him how much he got?
A Yes.

Q What did he say?
A Never made me any answer, walked right out.

Q Did you ever ask Charlie how much he got?
A Yes.

Q What did he say?
A Asked me how much I got.

Q What did you tell him?
A Told him.

Q What did you tell him?
A I told him I got $5,000.

Q What did he say?
A He said, "I guess that's all I got."

Q Did you believe him at the time?
A No, sir, I think he was telling a damn lie.

Q What?
A I think he was lying.

Q Did you tell him at the time he said it he was lying?
A Yes.

Q You thought he was lying even at that time, did you?
A Yes, sir.

Q When was that time?
A That was this spring. We were talking in Memphis, he and I were taking a walk.

Q On your training trip?
A Yes, sir.

Q Did you ever talk to anybody else about how much they got?
A No sir, I didn't.

Q You never asked Williams how much he got?
A Williams I have, yes.

Q What did he say?
A He said he got $5,000 at that time.

Q You think he gave you the truth?
A No, sir, I do not.

Q What do you say?
A No, I do not.

Q What do you think?
A I think that those fellers cut it up to suit themselves, what little they did have.

Q Who is this?
A This gang.

Q What gang?
A Charlie.

Q Charlie Risberg?
A Yes.

Q Who else?
A McMullin and Williams.

Q Who else?
A Cicotte, they were gambling.

Q Weren't you in on the inner circle?
A No, I never was with them, no, sir. It was mentioned to me in Boston. As I told you before, they asked me what would I consider, $10,000? And I said no, then they offered me twenty.

Q Who mentioned it first to you?
A Gandil.

Q Who was with you?
A We were all alone.

Q What did he say?
A He asked me would I consider $10,000 to frame up something and I asked him frame what? And he told me and I said no.

Q What did he say?
A Just walked away from me, and when I returned here to Chicago he told me that he would give me twenty and I said no again, and on the bridge where you go into the club house he told me I could either take it or let it alone, they were going through.

Q What did they say?
A They said, "You might as well say yes or say no and play ball or anything you want." I told them I would take their word."

Q What else did you say?
A Nothing.

Q Did you talk to anyone else about it?
A That's all I talked to.

Q Did you ever talk to Buck Weaver about it?
A No, sir, I never talked to Buck Weaver, never talked very much.

Q Did you know at the time Buck was in on the deal?
A They told me he was; he never told me it himself.

Q Who told you?
A Chick told me.

Q Did Mrs. Jackson ever talk to Mrs. Weaver about it, that you know of?
A No, sir, not that I know of; no, sir.

Q Is Mrs. Jackson a friend of Mrs. Weaver's, and did they chum together frequently—or did they?

A They are all chummy there on the ball ground, sit together there on the stand, most all the ballplayers' wives sit together.

Q Who did Mrs. Jackson sit with most?

A Mrs. Williams and her sit together.

Q Did Mrs. Jackson talk to Mrs. Williams about it?

A Not that I know of.

Q Did Mrs. Williams ever talk to Mrs. Jackson about it?

A I don't know, they never talked when I was around, I don't know what they did when I wasn't around.

Q Go back to Attell and Burns, just what do you know about them?

A All I know is what Gandil told me over there, I talked to Bill myself later.

Q When did you talk to Burns later?

A It was the day the World's Series started.

Q What did you say to him and what did he say to you?

A I met him in the lobby of the hotel, we sat there; I can't remember the name of the hotel.

Q Sinton Hotel?

A Sinton Hotel, yes.

Q That is in Cincinnati?

A Yes. I said, "How is everything?"

Q What did he say?

A He said, "Everything is fine."

Q Then what happened?

A He told me about this stuff and I didn't know so much, I hadn't been around and I didn't know so much. He said, "Where is Chick?" I said, "I don't know." He walked away from me. I didn't know enough to talk to him about what they were going to plan or what they had planned, I wouldn't know it if I had seen him, I only knew what I had been told, that's all I knew.

Q Who was the third party in with Burns and Attell?
A I don't know their names, I know there was three names.
THE FOREMAN:

Q What made you think that Gandil was double-crossing you, rather than Attell and Burns?
A What made me think it was, Gandil going out on the coast, so I was told, I was surmising what I heard, they came back and told me he had a summer home, big automobile, doesn't do a lick of work; I know I can't do that way.
MR. REPLOGLE:

Q In other words, if he double crossed you fellows he couldn't come back and face them, and he had plenty of money to stay out there. It wasn't at the time that you thought Gandil was double crossing you, you thought Gandil was telling the truth, is that right?
A No, I told Williams after the first day it was a crooked deal all the way through, Gandil was not on the square with us.

Q Had you ever played crooked baseball before this?
A No, sir, I never had.

Q Did anybody ever approach you to throw a game before this?
A No, sir, never did.

Q Did anybody approach you to throw a game since that time, to throw the World's Series?
A No, sir.

Q Do you have any suspicion about the White Sox, any of the players throw any of the games this summer?
A Well, there have been some funny looking games, runs, I could have just my own belief about it, I wouldn't accuse the men.

Q Where at?
A A couple in New York, this last Eastern trip, looked bad, but I couldn't come out and open and bold and accuse anybody of throwing those games.

Q Who pitched?
A Williams got one awful beating up there, 25 to something there.

Q Who else?
A I don't remember whether Cicotte started the game there or not.

Q Do you remember that series you played in Boston? Last three straight games, did any of those games look suspicious to you?
A There was a lot of funny pitching, lot of walking.

Q Who was pitching those games?
A Kerr and Williams and Cicotte.

Q Was Kerr in on this any way, do you think?
A I don't think so.

Q Were any of the other six players in it except the ones we have mentioned?
A Not to my knowledge.

Q Do you remember the Washington series here the last time Washington played here, that you lost three straight games?
A No, sir.

Q Did any of those games look suspicious to you?
A I didn't pay any attention to them, looking for errors, and that, I was out trying to beat them.

Q Was anything whispered around the club that you know of, that you should beat New York and then drop these games for these other teams so that Cleveland would win?
A No, sir, I never heard that.

Q Did you hear anything in your ball team to the effect that if the White Sox would take second place and would get part of the World's Series money because you won second place in the pennant race and then get the City Series money, that you would make more money than if you won the pennant and won the World's Series?
A No, sir.

Q Did any of the players ever tell you that?
A No, sir, never told me that.

Q Did that ever occur to you, yourself?
A No sir. I wanted to win, this year, above all times.

Q Why?
A Because—I wanted to get in there and try and beat some National League club to death, that's what I wanted to do.

Q You didn't want to do that so bad last year, did you?
A Well, down in my heart I did, yes.

Q Did you hear any of the players that mentioned that proposition to you that I have just mentioned?
A No, not to me, no, sir; they have not.

Q Have you heard from Gandil since he has been on the coast, has he written to you?
A No, sir.

Q Did you write and ask him for the other $15,000?
A No, sir.

Q Why didn't you?
A I didn't think it would do any good, I didn't pay any attention to that.

Q Did you ever talk to Claude Williams about it since the series?
A We have talked about it once or twice, yes.

Q When?
A Sometime this summer, I don't remember whom it was.

Q In what city, if you can recall?
A I think it was here, in Chicago.

Q Where in Chicago, at the ball park?
A No, we were out riding in his car.

Q What did you say to him and what did he say to you?
A We were just talking about how funny it looked that Gandil didn't come back, and he must have made an awful lot out of it, crossed up the boys. We both decided he crossed them up.

Q You think now Williams may have crossed you, too?
A Well, dealing with crooks, you know, you get crooked every way. This is my first experience and last.

Q Where else did you talk to Williams, outside of the time you were out riding in his car?
A Somewhere we were at, I believe in Washington.

Q When was that?
A That was this summer, I think.

Q How long ago?
A I think it was the second Eastern trip.

Q What did you say to him at that time, and what did he say to you?
A We just brought up the World's Series, I told him what a damned fool I thought I was, and he was of the same opinion, so we just let it go at that.

Q Does your contract with the Sox Baseball team call for $6,000?
A $8,000.

Q What part of the money did you get when you were sold by Cleveland to Comiskey?
A I think they gave me $1,000 out of the sale.

Q That's all you got out of it, just $1,000?
A Yes.

Q Do you know how much Mr. Comiskey paid the Cleveland Club for you?
A I do not, no, sir.

Q You knew it was a big sum of money, did you?
A So they said.

Q You were satisfied with $8,000 a year, were you?
A That's all I could get out of them.

Q Did you get $8,000 in 1919?
A No, sir.

Q What did you get in that year, that was last year?

A   '19, I believe they gave me $6,000, last year.

Q   That is for the season, not for the year?
A   Yes, just the playing season, yes, sir.

Q   That also includes all your expenses on the trips, doesn't it?
A   Yes, sir.

Q   Railroad fare, board, room and so forth?
A   Railroad fare, room and board.

Q   You were pretty well satisfied with that, weren't you?
A   They wouldn't give me any more, that's all you could get. I was pretty lucky to get a contract like that with him when I came over here.

Q   What were you getting with Cleveland?
A   I was getting six the last year, and I had been in that automobile wreck, and it looked like I was through as a ball player.

Q   That automobile wreck in Cleveland?
A   Yes; I had my leg all tore up, my knee cap came out, it looked like I would be through as a ball player.

Q $6,000 is the most you ever got until this year, is that right? (No answer)

Q   Did you ever talk to any of the other men about this, now, that I have not asked you about?
A   No, sir.

Q   Do you know anything more about it than I have asked you?
A   No, sir, I don't believe I do.

Q   Can you think of anything else of importance that I have not asked you?
A   No, sir I don't believe I do.

Q   Can you think of anything else of importance that I have not asked you?
A   This other fellow, if I could think of his name, I can't think of his name.

Q   Did Cicotte ever tell you who paid him the money?

A He told me about somebody paying him money, yes; but I don't know their names, never did know any of their names, except Bill Burns and Abe Attell, that's the only two names that I know. I did not attend the meetings.

Q You say Williams gave you your money; what ball player paid Cicotte his money?
A These gamblers paid him, I think, all along, from what I learn.

Q Did Williams ever tell you who paid him?
A Never did.

Q Did you ever ask Williams where he got this $5,000?
A Yes.

Q What did he say?
A Up at Gandil's apartment, he said.

Q Have you ever talked to Burns since the World's Series?
A No, sir.

Q Do you know where he lives, where he is?
A No, sir, I do not.

Q You talked to Gedeon this summer?
A Yes; "Hello, how are you," and something like that.

Q Do you know whether or not Gedeon is in on the deal?
A No, sir, I do not.

Q Do you think he was?
A (No answer)

Q Does Williams know where you are now?
A I don't think so.
MR. REPLOGLE: It is an off day, no game today.

> *(Whereupon the Grand Jury adjourned to Wednesday, September 29, 1920, at 9:30 A.M.)*

Bibliography

Alexander, Charles C. *Ty Cobb*, New York: Oxford University Press, 1984.

Asinof, Eliot. *Eight Men Out: The Black Sox and the 1919 World Series*. New York: Holt, Rinehart and Winston, 1963.

——————. *The Baseball Encyclopedia* (Eighth Edition) New York: Macmillan, 1990.

Benson, Michael. *Ballparks of North America*, Jefferson, North Carolina: McFarland & Co., 1989.

Broeg, Bob and Miller, William J., Jr. *Baseball From a Different Angle*, South Bend, Indiana: Diamond Communications, Inc., 1988.

Charlton, James. *The Baseball Chronology*, New York: Macmillan, 1991.

Connor, Anthony J. *Voices from Cooperstown*, New York: Collier Books, 1982.

Frommer, Harvey. *Primitive Baseball*, New York: Atheneum, 1988.

Gipe, George. *The Last Time When*, New York: World Almanac Publications, 1981.

Greenberg, Eric Ralph. *The Celebrant*, New York: Everest House, 1983.

Gropman, Donald. *Say It Ain't So, Joe!* Boston: Little, Brown & Co., 1979.

Lieb, Fred. *Baseball As I Have Known It*, New York: A Tempo Star Book, 1977.

Lindberg, Richard. *Sox*, New York: Macmillan, 1984.

Luhrs, Victor. *The Great Baseball Mystery*, New York: A.S. Barnes, 1966.

Malamud, Bernard. *The Natural*, New York: Harcourt Brace Jovanovich, 1952.

Okkonen, Marc. *Baseball Uniforms of the Twentieth Century*, New York: Sterling Publishing Company, 1991.

Rader, Benjamin G. *American Sports*, Englewood Cliffs, N.J.: Prentice-Hall, Inc., 1983.

Reidenbaugh, Lowell. *Take Me Out to the Ball Park*, St. Louis: The Sporting News Publishing Company, 1983.

Seymour, Harold. *Baseball: The Golden Age*, New York: Oxford University Press, 1971.

Sowell, Mike. *The Pitch that Killed*, New York: Macmillan, 1989.

Voigt, David Quentin. *American Baseball Volume I,* University Park, Pa.: The Pennsylvania University Press, 1983.

Files of *The Sporting News, The Greenville News, The New York Times, The Chicago Tribune*.

Index

About the Author

Harvey Frommer has written 29 books and over 600 articles, mostly on sports subjects. The author of the classic *New York City Baseball: 1947–1957* and the bestselling *Throwing Heat,* Nolan Ryan's autobiography, he is a professor of English in the City University of New York. Together with his wife Myrna, he wrote *It Happened in the Catskills,* an oral history of the resort region. They are currently at work on another oral history—this one dealing with Brooklyn, New York, in the postwar years. Harvey Frommer lives with his family in North Woodmere, Long Island.